Comptroller of the Currency
Administrator of National Banks

I0448291

Depository Services

Comptroller's Handbook

August 2010

CCE

Consumer Compliance Examination

Depository Services

Introduction

This booklet provides background information and optional expanded examination procedures for the following consumer protection regulations:

- Reserve Requirements of Depository Institutions;

- Electronic Fund Transfers;

- Interest on Deposits;

- Expedited Funds Availability; and

- Truth in Savings.

This booklet provides a synopsis of each regulation. Because the synopses are not comprehensive, users of this booklet should refer to each regulation for more detailed guidance and specific requirements.

Examiners will select from the procedures those that are necessary, if any, after first completing a compliance core assessment.

Reserve Requirements of Depository Institutions

Background and Summary

Section 19 of the Federal Reserve Act gives the Federal Reserve Board authority to impose reserve requirements on deposits of member institutions for monetary policy purposes and to define terms such as deposit, savings deposit, time deposit, nonpersonal time deposit, and transaction account.

The Monetary Control Act of 1980 (Title I of Pub. L. 96-221; 94 Stat. 132), which was enacted on March 31, 1980, imposes reserve requirements on depository institutions that maintain transaction accounts or nonpersonal time deposits. Effective November 13, 1980, the Board of Governors of the Federal Reserve System adopted a revised Regulation D to implement the provisions of that act.

Affected Institutions

Generally, depository institutions that maintain transaction accounts and nonpersonal time deposits are subject to Federal Reserve requirements. The term *depository institutions* encompasses:

- Any federally insured commercial or savings bank, or any commercial or savings bank that is eligible to be insured by the Federal Deposit Insurance Corporation (FDIC);

- Any mutual or stock savings bank;

- Any savings and loan association that is a member of a Federal Home Loan Bank and that is insured by, or is eligible to apply for insurance with, the FDIC;

- Any credit union that is insured by, or is eligible to apply for insurance with, the National Credit Union Administration Board;

- United States branches and agencies of foreign banks whose total worldwide consolidated bank assets are greater than $1 billion or that are eligible to apply for FDIC insurance; and

- Edge Act and agreement corporations (12 CFR 204.1(c)).

Computation of Reserves

Section 204.3 of Regulation D sets out the rules for computing the amount of reserves that must be held and the methods for holding them. It also permits carryover of certain reserve excesses and deficiencies and specifies pass-through rules. The *Reserve Maintenance Manual* also sets out the fundamental rules of reserve calculation and account maintenance for institutions that file the Report of Transaction Accounts, Other Deposits and Vault Cash (FR 2900) either weekly or quarterly. This manual is available on the Federal Reserve's financial services Web site (www.frbservices.org).

Exemption From Reserve Requirements

To provide relief from the reserve requirement to small depository institutions, the Garn-St Germain Depository Institutions Act of 1982 (Pub. L. 97-320; 96 Stat. 1520) exempted from reserve requirements the first $2 million of reservable liabilities of each depository institution.

Classification of Accounts

Regulation D defines deposit types under two main categories: transaction accounts and time deposit accounts.

Transaction Accounts

Transaction accounts permit unlimited third-party transfers and require a relatively large reserve requirement. They include demand deposit accounts (DDA), negotiable order of withdrawal (NOW) accounts, automatic transfer service (ATS) accounts, and telephone transfer accounts. Telephone transfer and DDA accounts are available to anyone. Eligibility requirements for NOW and ATS accounts are established by statute as follows:

- ATS accounts must consist only of funds in which the entire beneficial interest is held by one or more individuals.

- NOW accounts must consist only of funds in which the entire beneficial interest is held by one or more individuals or by a nonprofit organization operated primarily for religious, philanthropic, charitable, educational, political, or other similar purposes, such as political subdivisions, states, other government units, etc.

Time Deposit Accounts

Time deposit accounts either limit or prohibit third-party transfers and currently do not require reserves. Available to anyone, time deposit accounts include savings accounts, money market deposit accounts (MMDAs), IBF (International banking facility) time deposits and borrowings held in foreign countries, and special time-deposit accounts that require a minimum seven-day maturity period and the imposition of limited early withdrawal penalties.

Regulation D also includes a separate category for nonpersonal time deposits. A *nonpersonal time deposit* is defined as (1) a transferable time deposit or account or (2) a time deposit or account representing funds deposited to the credit of, or in which any beneficial interest is held by, a depositor that is not a natural person (12 CFR 204.2(f)). The term *natural person* includes an individual or sole proprietorship but does not apply to partnerships, corporations (including one solely owned by an individual), governmental units, or other associations or organizations (12 CFR 204.2(g)). Although nonpersonal time deposits (including applicable savings deposits) are subject to reserve requirements, there is currently no reserve requirement imposed on them.

NOTE: Any deposit failing to meet the definition of either a *time deposit* or a *savings deposit* is considered a *transaction account* subject to reserve requirements for transaction accounts. For example, if the depositor is authorized to exceed the transfer limits applicable to savings deposits or MMDAs, such accounts would be transaction accounts for the purposes of Regulation D and subject to larger reserve requirements. However, these accounts would not be demand deposits for the purposes of the interest payment prohibition of Regulation Q, if the depositor is eligible to hold another type of account, such as a NOW and ATS account, that would permit the particular excess transfers. For other depositors, savings deposits and MMDAs authorized to exceed the withdrawal or transfer limits would be considered demand deposits on which interest could not be paid.

Regulation D Deposit Requirements

Transaction Accounts

All Accounts
Current maximum reserve requirement imposed:
10 percent, effective April 2, 1992.
Unlimited third-party transfers.
No early withdrawal penalties.
No minimum balance requirement.

Demand Deposit Accounts (DDAs)
Available to anyone.

Include any of the following:
- Payable on demand.
- Issued with an original maturity of less than seven days.
- Issued without the bank reserving its right to require at least seven days' written notice of intended withdrawal.

Interest is prohibited.

NOW Accounts
No business accounts.

Unrestricted interest rate.

Bank must reserve right to require seven-day depositor notice of withdrawal.

ATS Accounts
Natural persons only.

Unrestricted interest rate.

Bank must reserve its right to require seven-day depositor notice of withdrawal.

Unlimited automatic transfers to bank or DDAs.

Telephone Transfer Accounts
Available to anyone.

Unrestricted interest rate for depositors eligible to hold NOW accounts.

Bank must reserve its right to require seven-day depositor notice of withdrawal.

Not included in this category:
- Withdrawals and other than third-party transfers.
- Transfers and withdrawals that conform to NOW and ATS account requirements.

Time Deposits

All Accounts
Current maximum reserve requirement imposed:
None.
Unrestricted interest rate.
Available to anyone.
No minimum balance requirements.

Savings Accounts
Bank must reserve the right to require seven-day depositor notice of withdrawal.

Depositor is not required by the deposit contract to give written notice of intended withdrawal.

Money Market Deposit Accounts (MMDAs)
Unlimited withdrawals permitted if:
- Done in person, by messenger, by mail, or at an ATM.
- Made by telephone when a check is mailed to the depositor.

Unlimited transfers are permitted:
- Between accounts of the same depositor at the same bank, provided transfer is done in person, by messenger, by mail, or at an ATM.
- To pay loans at the same bank.

Up to six transfers a month permitted to another account of the depositor at the same bank or to third party if by preauthorized, automatic, or telephone agreement. Three of the six transfers may be by check, draft, or debit card. NOTE: If the transaction limits are exceeded, the account becomes a transaction account.

Other Time Deposits (e.g., CDs)
Minimum seven-day maturity.

No third-party transaction.

To qualify as a time deposit, a certificate of deposit must be subject to a minimum early withdrawal penalty — seven days simple interest if withdrawn within six days of the date of deposit or date of last withdrawal.

NOTE: For reporting purposes only, other time deposits are normally classified as short-term deposits. If the deposit has a maturity of 18 months or more and one month's simple interest early withdrawal penalty is imposed for withdrawals made between day seven and the end of month 18, instead of the normal seven days penalty, the deposit may be classified as a long-term deposit.

Federal Reserve Board Staff Opinions and Rulings: Regulation D

The staff opinions and rulings below address Regulation D, Reserve Requirements of Depository Institutions. They provide guidance for compliance with Regulation D.

NOW Account Eligibility

Individuals Operating Businesses

A husband and wife operating a profit-making business as individuals, but not as a partnership or other financial business organization, may maintain a NOW account at a member bank, because it is impracticable to distinguish between funds that are used in their business and other funds of those individuals. STAFF OP. of January 23, 1979. *Authority: 12 CFR 204.130.*

International Organizations and Foreign Governmental Units

Agencies of a foreign government may not maintain NOW accounts, because the beneficial interest in their funds remains with the foreign government, which is organized primarily for foreign government purposes. A consulate or embassy of a foreign government may not maintain NOW accounts, because the beneficial interest in the funds deposited by such consulates is with the government it represents. Federal law (12 U.S.C. 1832(a)) provides that only domestic governmental units are eligible to maintain NOW accounts. Similarly, U.N. officers (embassy staff) may not maintain NOW accounts if the funds deposited are funds of the United Nations or funds in which any beneficial interest is held by the United Nations, because the primary purpose of the organization is not charitable, fraternal, or educational (even though an element of a fraternal purpose is evidenced by the charter). STAFF OP. of March 5, 1979. *Authority: 12 CFR 204.130.*

Professionals

Professionals operating on an unassociated basis are among the class of depositors eligible to maintain NOW accounts, because it is impracticable to distinguish between funds used in their individual and business capacity. Professionals operating as partnerships or corporations, however, are not eligible, since Congress intended that NOW accounts be made available only to individuals, and funds of such business organizations would always be used for business purposes. STAFF OP. of May 1, 1979. *Authority: 12 CFR 204.130.*

Beneficiary of Attorney Trust Fund

The question has been raised whether attorney trust funds may be deposited in interest-bearing NOW accounts at member banks when the funds are maintained under the interest on lawyer trust account (IOLTA).

Section 303 of the Consumer Checking Account Equity Act of 1980 (Title III of Pub. L. 96-221) provides the following test of eligibility for NOW accounts: (1) the account must consist solely of funds in which the entire beneficial interest is held by one or more individuals, by a governmental unit, or by an organization operated primarily for religious, philanthropic, charitable, educational, or other similar purposes; and (2) the organization must not be operated for profit (12 USC 1832(a)). The Federal Reserve Board regards this provision as including organizations not operated for profit that are described in section 501(c)(3) of the Internal Revenue Code.

In determining whether client funds may be deposited in NOW accounts under IOLTA programs, the Board has required (1) evidence that the organization administering the program is either a governmental unit or a nonprofit organization operated for religious, philanthropic, charitable, educational, or other similar purposes eligible for tax-exempt status under section 501(c)(3) of the Internal Revenue Code; and (2) an opinion from the appropriate state attorney general that the organization involved holds the beneficial interest in the accounts because it has the exclusive right to the interest on the funds maintained in the program. STAFF OP. of November 5, 1984. *Authority: Consumer Checking Account Equity Act 303, 12 USC 1832; IRC §501(c)(3), 26 USC 501(c)(3).*

Husband-and-Wife Partnership

A husband-and-wife partnership is not eligible to maintain a NOW account at a member bank. Eligibility for NOW accounts is established by 12 USC 1832(a), which authorizes institutions to offer NOW accounts. Paragraph (2) of that section specifically excludes for-profit partnerships. Although a husband-and-wife for-profit partnership cannot maintain a NOW account, a husband and wife are permitted to maintain a joint NOW account for their nonpartnership purposes. STAFF OP. of October 16, 1986. *Authority: Consumer Checking Account Equity Act 303(a), 12 USC 1832(a); 12 CFR 204.130.*

U.S. Embassies of Foreign Governments

Embassies of foreign governments are not eligible to maintain NOW accounts at member banks under Board interpretation 12 CFR 204.130. That interpretation states that governmental units are generally eligible to maintain NOW accounts at member banks and is based on the statute authorizing depository institutions to offer NOW accounts (12 USC 1832(a)).

The Garn-St Germain Depository Institutions Act of 1982 amended 12 USC 1832(a) to extend eligibility to certain governmental units. The statutory language clearly extends eligibility for NOW accounts only to deposits of public funds of listed entities. Further, the legislative history confirms that the amendment was intended to extend eligibility only to domestic, Commonwealth, and territorial governmental units (see Conf. Rep. (S. Rep.) No. 641, 97th Cong., 2d Sess. (1982), at 92; S. Rep. No. 536, 97th Cong., 2d Sess., (1982), at 44). NOW account eligibility cannot be extended to governmental units other than those listed in this interpretation. STAFF OP. of August 19, 1987. *Authority: Consumer Checking Account Equity Act 303(a), 12 USC 1832(a); 12 CFR 204.130.*

Attorney Trust Accounts Other Than IOLTA

A question was raised about the legality of a depository institution's establishing a NOW account to hold trust funds for a law firm other than under the programs known as interest on lawyer trust accounts (IOLTAs). This proposed account would be established in the name of the law firm that is a partnership composed of professional associations. The law firm would have an interest in approximately 35 percent of the deposited funds, but interest earned on the funds would inure to the benefit of clients of the firm, and these clients would all be natural persons.

In the situation described, the law firm would have an interest in the deposited funds even though it would not have an interest in the interest earned on the funds. Because the law firm is a partnership, the account would not consist "solely of funds in which the entire beneficial interest is held by one or more individuals." Therefore, the account would not qualify as a NOW account. STAFF OP. of July 25, 1988. *Authority: Consumer Checking Account Equity Act 303(a), 12 USC 1832(a); 12 CFR 204.130.*

Student Loan Accounts

Department of Education regulations concerning student loan programs require participating institutions to set up a Perkins Loan Fund containing student loan monies, which must be maintained in interest-bearing accounts. The participating institution does not have the right to receive any of the income generated by assets in the account, which remain the property of the loan fund. Income from the account is considered to be held in trust for the Department of Education, and the account holder is not taxed on that income.

In general, interest may not be paid on demand deposits except for NOW accounts, which may be held only by individuals, certain not-for-profit organizations, or governmental units. Schools that operate on a for-profit basis are not eligible for NOW accounts. In the past, ineligible persons or entities have been permitted to deposit funds into NOW accounts in connection with IOLTA programs. Student loan program accounts are eligible for similar treatment. In determining whether to issue a favorable opinion letter to an IOLTA program, the Board has used the following criteria: (1) evidence that the beneficiary of the interest from the NOW accounts is either a 501(c)(3) organization under the Internal Revenue Code or is a governmental unit; and (2) an attorney general's opinion that the organization or unit holds the entire beneficial interest in the account because it has the exclusive right to the interest earned on the account, or a similar statutory provision. In this case, the beneficial interest in the funds would be considered to be held by individuals or by the United States government, either of which would be eligible to hold a NOW account. STAFF OP. of February 28, 1989. Authority: 20 USC 1087cc(a)(3); FRA 19(i), 12 USC 371a; Consumer Checking Account Equity Act 303, 12 USC 1832.

Savings Deposits

Totten Trust

A savings account is often used as a vehicle for a Totten trust, a tentative, revocable trust that is created by the deposit of one's own money as a trustee for another with a presumption that title passes on the death of the trustee. The question has arisen whether the money market deposit account (MMDA) is suitable for use as a Totten trust in the same manner as a regular savings account. Regulation D treats an MMDA as a type of savings account, and Board staff is aware of no federal law that would prohibit the use of an

MMDA as a vehicle for a Totten trust. However, private counsel should be consulted to determine whether, under state law, an MMDA is an appropriate vehicle by which to establish a Totten trust. STAFF OP. of April 7, 1983. *Authority: 12 CFR 204.2(d)(2)(ii).*

Preauthorized Transfers from MMDA

The question has arisen whether an arrangement whereby a depository institution sends an employee to a customer's place of business to receive authorization to make a transfer from the MMDA to another account of the depositor at the same institution would be regarded as a transfer subject to the limit of six preauthorized or automatic transfers per month. Such transfers are regarded as preauthorized transfers and therefore subject to the six-per-month limitation. STAFF OP. of June 27, 1983. *Authority: 12 CFR 204.2(d)(2).*

Withdrawals by Messenger

A bank offers an account arrangement in which a corporation opens a zero-balance checking account and a MMDA. At the same time, the corporation enters into a messenger agreement and authorization with a messenger service and the bank. The messenger service is not owned or controlled by, or otherwise affiliated with the bank. Under the messenger agreement, the corporation authorizes the messenger to deliver to the bank instructions to make transfers from the corporation's MMDA to its checking account. The authorization also indicates that the messenger is authorized to receive information confirming transactions from the bank and transmit it to the customer. The bank absorbs the expense associated with the messenger service.

A customer is permitted to write checks on its zero-balance checking account. At the beginning of the day, the bank determines the amount of checks that had been presented to it for payment the previous day. The messenger calls the bank daily and is told the amount that must be transferred from the customer's MMDA to its checking account to cover the checks presented. The messenger service then prepares a transfer instruction and delivers it to the bank. Upon receipt of the instruction, the bank makes the transfer. The bank is unaware of whether the messenger service consults with the customer before the instruction is initiated; however, such a consultation is not required. Interest is paid by the bank on the balance maintained in the

MMDA on a sliding scale, depending on the level of balances maintained. A 3 percent reserve is maintained against the balances in the MMDA.

The purpose of the exception for withdrawals or transfers by messenger in the MMDA rules was to recognize that a depositor could appear in person or through an agent to effect the transactions. This exception was adopted after the Board balanced the hardships and burdens that could result if such withdrawals were limited against the potential risk that such transactions would be used to evade the six preauthorized withdrawals limitation. The Board believed that depositors who made withdrawals in person or through a messenger ordinarily would not use the arrangement to avoid the six-withdrawal limitation because the depositor would be required either to appear physically at the bank or establish an arrangement with a messenger. It was never contemplated that the bank itself would be involved in establishing and maintaining the arrangement. Further, it was understood that the depositor would be involved in the initiation of each transfer instruction, as is ordinarily the case.

The arrangement is inconsistent with the language and intent of the Board's regulations relating to the operation of MMDAs and is contrary to federal law and regulation for several reasons. First, the arrangement appears to be a device to avoid the prohibition against payment of interest on demand deposits because it results in the payment of interest on demand balances maintained to cover checks drawn on a corporate customer's checking account. Second, because of the bank's involvement in establishing and maintaining the relationship with the messenger service, the arrangement violates the limitation of six preauthorized transfers contained in Regulations D and Q. The bank absorbs the cost of the messenger and, in making daily transfers, deals virtually exclusively with the messenger rather than with the customer of the bank. It is apparent that the messenger is more an agent of the bank than of the customer, and that the messenger agreement serves no purpose other than to assist in evasion of the limitation of six preauthorized transfers per month. The transfers, therefore, appear to be automatic and prearranged, particularly since there is no apparent requirement for contact between the messenger and the customer for authorization of each transfer. Finally, there is no indication that the bank imposes any charges or interest on the overdraft in the demand deposit account to which transfers are made, as required by board regulations.

It is apparent that the sole purpose of the arrangement is to enable businesses to earn interest on their checking account balances. The program therefore violates Regulations D and Q because it results in the payment of interest on demand deposits and because the bank does not maintain transaction account reserves against balances in the MMDA accounts. Consequently, the bank was advised to cease offering the program to new customers and to terminate the accounts it had already established as soon as possible. STAFF OP. of November 16, 1984. *Authority: 12 CFR 204.2(d)(2)(i) and (ii), 204.2(b), and 217.2.*

Money Market Deposit Accounts

A bank proposes to offer MMDAs and to provide overdraft protection on these accounts under an arrangement by which the bank will transfer funds into the accounts to cover debits against the accounts in excess of the account balances. Transfers out of each MMDA will be restricted to not more than six per month.

Because transfers from each MMDA will be limited to not more than six per month (no more than three of which will be by check, draft, or similar order), the status of the accounts as MMDAs will not be affected by overdraft protection. In the questions and answers to Regulation D, the Board has said that the status of a savings account is not affected by the nature of transfers made into the account. Because MMDAs are savings deposits, that principle applies to MMDAs.

In limiting transfers from MMDAs, section 204.2(d)(2)(ii) states that an account is not a transaction account by virtue of an arrangement that "permits transfers for the purpose of repaying loans and associated expenses at the same depository institution (as originator or servicer)." When third-party transfers from each MMDA are limited to six per month, the satisfaction of the loans created as a result of overdraft protection constitutes the repayment of loans to the depository institution that originated the loans. Consequently, the repayment of those loans from MMDAs by means of preauthorized transfers will not count toward the six-transfer limit. STAFF OP. of September 2, 1988. *Authority: 12 CFR 204.2(d)(2)(ii).*

MMDAs on Escrow Accounts

Regulations of the Department of Transportation specify that a depository agreement must be executed among a bank, an air carrier, and a tour operator, and must provide for the return of funds to charter-flight participants if certain conditions are not met. A bank proposes to place the escrowed funds attributable to each tour operator in one MMDA per operator. Each tour operator may have 20 to 30 charter trips scheduled over a given period and will need to make at least three withdrawals by telephone transfer or by check per trip. Several of the 20 to 30 charter trips will be scheduled to depart each month, thus necessitating more than six transfers from each MMDA monthly.

Section 204.2(d)(2)(ii) of Regulation D defines an MMDA as:

The number of permissible transfers is not affected by the number of beneficial holders of the account. Insofar as the transfer restrictions are concerned, the bank must look solely to the number of transfers permitted or authorized for the account. If that number exceeds six, the account does not qualify as an MMDA. In the arrangement described, the bank proposes to establish one MMDA for each tour operator and not one per individual. Because more than six transfers per month will be made from the account, it will not qualify as an MMDA.

The types of depository agreements described cannot qualify as interest-bearing transaction accounts such as NOW accounts because the accounts will be held by profit-making entities (i.e., the tour operators) and the air carriers are beneficiaries of the accounts. (By statute, beneficial ownership is relevant for determining eligibility for a NOW account (see 12 USC 1832(a)). These funds could be placed in demand deposit accounts. However, unlike MMDAs and NOW accounts, demand deposit accounts may not pay interest. STAFF OP. of August 24, 1987. *Authority: 12 CFR 204.2(d)(2)(ii).*

MMDAs — Monitoring of Transfers

A depository institution proposes to offer a money market deposit account monitored to discourage withdrawals or transfers in excess of those permissible for MMDAs. The monitoring system would look to consecutive months in which there were transfer violations. After the first month in which there were excess transfers, the institution would send a letter reminding the customer of the transfer limit and informing the customer that the limit was exceeded. If excess transfers were made during the next month, the institution would send a letter informing the customer of the violation and stating that continued violation would result in elimination of the transfer capacity or conversion of the account to a checking account. If the depositor exceeded the transfer limit for a third consecutive month, the institution would send a letter informing the customer that the account has been converted to a transaction account.

The proposed monitoring system would fail to ensure that there are no more than six transfers per month and fail to ensure that there are no more than three transfers by check, draft, debit card, or similar order per month. A depositor could make unlimited transfers from the account for three consecutive months before the institution would close the account. For example, a customer could write 20 checks per week on its account in the first month. Only after the end of the month would the customer receive a reminder of the transfer limit. This transfer activity could continue through the second month, when the customer would receive another warning. Only after the third consecutive month of such activity would the account be changed to a transaction account.

If an account becomes a transaction account as defined in section 204.2(e) because of excess transfers, then Regulation CC, Availability of Funds and Collection of Checks (12 CFR 229), would also apply. STAFF OP. of December 6, 1988. *Authority: 12 CFR 204.2(d)(1) and (2)*.

Terminals Authorizing Cash Disbursement by Retailer

The question was raised whether the use in retail outlets of electronic terminals that authorize transactions, including the disbursement of cash by the retail outlets, would result in withdrawals from an automated teller machine (ATM) rather than third-party transfers by debit card, particularly under section 204.2(d)(2) of Regulation D.

A depository institution proposes to locate an electronic terminal on the premises of a retail merchant. The depository institution's customer would use this terminal to designate the account from which to withdraw funds, and the amount of the withdrawal. The terminal would authorize or reject the transaction, but would not disburse funds. Rather, the customer would take an authorization voucher produced by the terminal to a cashier's window on the merchant's premises, sign a receipt, and receive cash from the cashier. The customer would then be able to use the funds in any manner.

The term *savings deposit* includes deposits in savings accounts from which the depositor is permitted to make no more than three preauthorized or telephone (including computer) transfers per month. Savings deposit also includes accounts commonly known as money market deposit accounts

(MMDAs), from which the depositor is permitted to make no more than six preauthorized or telephone (including computer) transfers per month and from which three of the six transfers may be accomplished by check, draft, or debit card. Such an account is not a transaction account by virtue of an arrangement that permits withdrawals (payments directly to the depositor) from the account when such transfers or withdrawals are made at an ATM, regardless of the number of such transfers or withdrawals.

If the arrangement results in third-party transfers by debit card, the depository institution may permit only three such transfers per month from an MMDA. However, if the arrangement is treated as resulting in withdrawals from an ATM, no limit is placed on the number of withdrawals.

In discussing why transfers initiated at an ATM from one of the customer's accounts to another of the customer's accounts at the same depository institution, or why withdrawals paid directly to the customer do not count toward the permissible number of transfers and withdrawals from an MMDA, the Board has previously advised that "it is the character of the underlying transfer (that is, whether the payment initiated by the customer is made directly to the customer or the customer's account rather than to a third party or third-party's account) that determines whether the transfer counts in distinguishing between a savings and a transaction account."

The arrangement described above may be treated as resulting in withdrawals from an ATM, provided that the money will be paid directly to the customer. The dispensing of cash by personnel of the retail establishment, as opposed to through the terminal, does not so distinguish these transactions from withdrawals at an ATM as to warrant different treatment. In effect, staff of the retail establishment would be substituted for the cash-dispensing mechanism of an ATM.

It is important that customers be able to use the funds in any manner they choose. The retail establishment may not restrict the use of funds withdrawn by use of the terminal. It may not require that the funds be used for the purchase of goods or services from the retail establishment or for any other purpose.

Each depository institution from which such withdrawals are made should have an effective means of monitoring and policing the practices of the retail establishments in which the terminals are located to ensure that the establishments do not restrict the use of the funds. Such use of the terminals affects the status of the depository institution's deposit accounts, and improper practices on the part of a retail establishment could subject each depository institution not only to the reclassification of MMDAs or savings deposits to transaction or demand accounts under Regulation D, but also to penalties for violating Regulation Q if the accounts become demand deposits and interest is paid on them, and Regulation CC if appropriate disclosures and availability policies have not been followed.

This opinion addresses the Regulation D aspects of this program only and does not address other issues such as branch banking laws. STAFF OPs. of April 5, 1989, and August 1, 1989. *Authority: 204.2(d)(2).*

Monitoring Transfers from MMDAs

A bank proposes to compile monthly reports of customers who had excessive MMDA transactions the previous month, notify customers by letter regarding those excessive transfers, and close any account if the transfer limits were violated during four consecutive months.

These procedures would not result in compliance with the six-transfer limit on MMDAs. Footnote 5, referred to in footnote 6 of section 204.2(d)(2)(ii), requires institutions to monitor transfers and contact customers who exceed the limits more than occasionally.

Footnote 5 provides that the rule limiting transfers need not be applied mechanically, but it does not change the fundamental requirement that a depository institution may not permit or authorize more than six transfers from an MMDA per month. Thus, if the circumstances warrant, an institution may not be required to close or reclassify an MMDA in the event of an occasional excess transfer from the account. Enforcement procedures that focus on excess transfers in consecutive months and that ignore excess transfers in any particular month would not be sufficient to prevent excess transfers from MMDAs, and would therefore fail to meet the monitoring requirements of Regulation D.

Ideally, controls on excess transfers should be sufficiently flexible to address both excess transfers in nonconsecutive months as well as the level of excess transfers in a particular month. Such controls would help depository institutions distinguish inadvertent violations of the transfer limits from abuses of the transfer limits. Thus, when a customer ignores the transfer limits applicable to an MMDA, the depository institution should take steps to close the account more quickly than it would an account from which the depositor inadvertently, and occasionally, exceeds the transfer limits by a single transfer. Nevertheless, a monitoring system that would detect and prevent all excess transfers may be costly to administer. For this reason, the Board has applied a general rule that an institution may continue to consider an account an MMDA even if there are excess transfers so long as those excess transfers are not the result of an attempt to evade the transfer limits, and if the excess transfers occur in not more than three months during any 12-month period. This working rule is not absolute, however, and the facts and circumstances must be considered in each case.

The proposed standards for monitoring MMDAs would not adequately prevent excess transfers. They do not take into account the number of excess transfers in an MMDA in any one month; a large number may be evidence of an intent to evade the transfer limits. Further, the standards would permit excess transfers in four consecutive months. Therefore, the proposed standards could result in violations of the transfer restrictions on MMDAs. STAFF OP. of Feb. 15, 1990. *Authority: 12 CFR 204.2(d)(2).*

MMDA Transfer by Facsimile Machine

A bank proposes to offer a MMDA arrangement in which deposits would be placed in the MMDA from various sources, but daily transfers would be made to a customer's commercial checking account. Instructions to make the transfer and instructions on third-party payments to be made from the checking account would be transmitted to the bank by facsimile (fax) machine.

The stated intention of the arrangement was to allow the payment of a high rate of interest on the funds with little administrative work by the bank. MMDAs have restrictions on the number of transactions by check, preauthorized agreement, or telephone, but no restrictions apply to withdrawals made by mail, by messenger, or in person. The bank views instructions received by fax machine as functionally the same as instructions received by mail.

In order for a deposit to be considered an MMDA for purposes of Regulation D, it must be limited to no more than six transfers per calendar month or statement cycle of at least four weeks. Section 204.2(d)(2)(ii) explicitly provides that transfers to another account of the depositor at the same institution or to a third party count toward the limitation when transfers are made by preauthorized or automatic transfer or telephonic agreement (including data transmission), order, or instruction. Therefore, the use of fax machines to transmit interaccount transfer instructions constitutes a data transmission order or instruction via telephone. STAFF OP. of January 30, 1991. *Authority: 12 CFR 204.2(d)(2)(ii).*

Transfers for Overdraft Protection

The question has arisen whether transfers from a savings deposit to cover overdrafts on a checking account are subject to the three-check or six-transfer limit of Regulation D. If a deposit or account is maintained in connection with an overdraft arrangement under which transfers are made from a savings deposit to a transaction account to cover checks presented to the depository institution that exceed the balance in the account as those checks are presented, the transfers are subject to the six-transfer limit. On the other hand, if transfers are made from a savings deposit to repay prior credit that was extended by the bank to pay checks drawn on a transaction account, the transfers should be considered transfers to repay loans from the bank. In the former case, the use of the savings-deposit balance as a substitute for a transaction-account balance is effectively limited by the six-transfer limit. However, in the latter case, the savings-account balance could be a substitute for the transaction-account balance because the bank imposes no limit on the transfers to repay loans from the institution. Thus, overdraft protection arrangements involving extensions of credit must be reviewed to determine whether the savings accounts should be considered transaction accounts.

The factors determining whether these arrangements result in transaction accounts include the rates of interest charged on the outstanding balances under the lines of credit, the interest earned on the time deposits, the balances ordinarily maintained in the transaction accounts, the activity in the transaction accounts, the frequency with which advances on the lines of credit are satisfied from transfers from the savings deposits rather than other funds of the customer, and the extent that the depository institution suggests, promotes, or otherwise furthers the establishment of the arrangements. STAFF OP. of January 31, 1992. *Authority: 12 CFR 204.2(d)(2) and (e)(5).*

Monitoring of Transfers

A depository institution proposes the following system to monitor and enforce the transfer limits imposed on savings deposits. Whenever one to four transfers over the monthly maximum have occurred, a first notice would be sent to remind the customer of the prohibition against excess transfers or withdrawals. A second notice containing a strong message that excessive transfers or withdrawals will result in conversion of the account to a non-interest-bearing transaction account would be sent whenever any of the following occurred: five to fourteen transfers over the maximum in any month; three to four transfers over the monthly maximum in any two months out of the past 12 months; or three first notices in any 12-month period. Finally, if four first notices in any 12-month period or three second notices in a 12-month period have been sent, or if 15 or more transfers over the monthly maximum in any one month have been made, the depository institution would review the 12-month account history, including an averaging test, to determine whether there has been an attempt to evade the transfer limits. The depository institution would examine the average number of transfers per month to determine if the excess transfers result from the lack of customer control over the timing of negotiation of the checks or drafts (or bunching). If the review does not reveal lack of intent to evade or extenuating circumstances, then the depository institution would give third and final notice that the account had been converted to a non-interest-bearing transaction account.

The proposed monitoring system would not adequately ensure compliance with the transfer limits imposed in section 204.2(d)(2) of Regulation D. For example, a customer could have 14 transfers over the monthly maximum and receive only a second warning rather than have the account closed or reclassified. The customer could accrue three such second warnings before the account was closed or reclassified. This arrangement permits customers materially to exceed the transfer limits for savings deposits.

Footnote 5 to Regulation D requires depository institutions that do not prevent excess transfers to monitor transfers from savings deposits to ensure that customers do not use these accounts as substitutes for transaction accounts. Monitoring systems that do not strictly limit the number of transfers to the permissible levels should be designed to enable the institution to consider the probable causes of excess transfers so that it can take appropriate action. If an institution monitors a savings account during a month and notifies a customer of transfers in excess of the transfer limits promptly after the excess transfers are discovered, the customer may take appropriate steps to prevent additional excess transfers during the remainder of the month, and the institution may not need to close the account or take other remedial action. On the other hand, if monitoring is performed and notice is given only after the close of the month, the customer who has exceeded the transfer limits early in the statement cycle might have a significant number of additional transfers during the month that will far exceed the transfer limits.

The monitoring and notice provisions of footnote 5 are intended to be used by depository institutions to give customers an opportunity to revise their transfer practices before the institution must take remedial action. They are not intended to expand the number of transfers that could be made from a savings deposit. STAFF OP. of February 11, 1992. *Authority: 12 CFR 204.2(d)(2).*

Six-Transfer Limit

The question has arisen whether a check that is deposited into a savings account and subsequently returned and charged back against the account must be considered one of the six transfers per month permitted under Regulation D.

When a check is returned unpaid to a depository institution that had received the check as a deposit to a savings account and had provided credit for the deposit to its customer, the depository institution may charge the check back to the customer's account and that charge would not count as a transfer and therefore would not count toward the six-transfer limit applicable to savings accounts. STAFF OP. of July 29, 1992. *Authority: 12 CFR 204.2(d).*

Transfer Restrictions

Several questions have arisen concerning the transfer limits on savings deposits in section 204.2(d)(2) of Regulation D. Although the questions refer to savings and money market accounts as separate types of accounts, Regulation D no longer makes this distinction. (See 56 Fed. Reg. 15493 at 15494, April 17, 1991.)

Question 1: A savings account is used for overdraft protection for checks drawn on a demand deposit account. Does the six-transfer limit apply to overdraft transfers? Are transfers to cover overdrafts created as a result of credit card, ATM, and automated clearing house (ACH) transactions subject to the six-transfer limit?

Regulation D defines savings deposit in 204.2(d)(2) and transaction account in section 204.2(e). Overdraft protection can be accomplished by directly transferring funds from a savings account to pay charges to the account or by posting those charges to a line of credit. In some cases, however, it is accomplished by a combination of these methods: a line of credit is extended to the customer and drawings on the line of credit are satisfied by preauthorized transfers from a savings account.

A transfer from a savings deposit to repay a bona fide loan from the bank resulting from overdraft protection does not count as a transfer subject to the transfer limit. Depending on the facts and circumstances, section 204.2(e)(5) might apply to an arrangement under which a depository institution allows a customer to have draws on a line of credit to pay overdrafts on an account and then allows the customer to satisfy those draws by transfers from a savings deposit. If section 204.2(e)(5) applies, the savings deposit will be reclassified as a transaction account.

Generally, if by arrangement transfers are made from a savings account to a transaction account, each transfer to the transaction account counts toward the six-transfer limit in section 204.2(d)(2). In that case, the use of the savings-account balance as a substitute for a transaction-account balance is effectively limited by the six-transfer limit. However, if the transfers from the savings account are used to repay credit extended to the holder of the transaction account because of overdrafts, the arrangement also must be analyzed under section 204.2(e)(5) because the extension of credit, in conjunction with the transfers, may increase the depositor's ability to substitute savings-account balances for transaction-account balances. In these cases, a savings account may be considered a transaction account even though fewer than six transfers per month are made from the savings account.

In determining whether a line-of-credit overdraft arrangement involving transfers from a savings account results in the savings account being considered a transaction account under section 204.2(e)(5), one must consider all the facts and circumstances, including the rates of interest charged on the outstanding balance under the line of credit; the interest rate earned on the savings account; the balance ordinarily maintained in the transaction account; the activity in the transaction account; the frequency with which advances on the line of credit are satisfied from transfers from the savings account rather than other funds from the customer; and the extent to which the depository institution suggests, promotes, or otherwise furthers the establishment of the arrangement.

The Board also has been asked whether transfers to cover overdrafts created as a result of credit card, ATM, and ACH transactions are subject to the six-transfer limit. A credit card transaction is a transaction by which credit is extended to the cardholder. Although credit extended by means of a credit card may be paid by means of a transfer from a savings account, the individual credit card transactions would not ordinarily count as transfers from the savings deposit. A debit card, however, does access an account directly, and debits from a savings account by means of a debit card are limited to three per month. ACH transactions on a savings account are subject to the six-transfer limit. ATM cash withdrawals or transfers from a savings deposit to another account of the depositor at the same depository institution are neither subject to the three- nor six-transfer limit.

Question 2: If four checks are overdrawn against an overdraft-protected demand deposit account on the same day, should the system count one or four transfers if (1) the processing system used by the bank transfers funds for each check, or (2) the system sums the four checks and makes one transfer to cover all four checks?

These transactions are governed by section 204.2(d)(2), which limits transfers from a savings account to another account of the depositor at the same institution to six per month. Generally, each separate transfer from a savings account to a transaction account should be counted against the transfer limit. If four checks are processed separately (for example, when each check is presented to the institution at a different time during the day for payment over the counter in cash) and the bank transfers funds from the customer's savings account to the customer's transaction account at the time each check is paid, then the savings account would be charged with four transfers. Likewise, if transfers from a checking account would result in overdrafts and a separate transfer from the savings account to the checking account would be made to cover each funds transfer, then each transfer from the savings account would count toward the six-transfer limit. The making of separate transfers to cover individual checks, even if the checks were presented together, ordinarily would result in separate transfers for purposes of the transfer limit, unless the depository institution could demonstrate that the separation of the transfers was wholly unrelated to the separate payment of checks. If, however, the checks that are presented on the transaction account are processed in a batch rather than individually, and only one transfer equal to the sum of the overdrafts is made from the savings account, then only one transfer from the savings deposit need be charged against the transfer limit.

If a transfer is made from a savings deposit to repay a prior extension of credit by the bank and the credit was extended to pay checks drawn on a transaction account, the transfer generally would be considered a transfer to repay the loan from the bank and usually would not count toward the six-transfer limit. In that case, however, the savings-account balance could be a substitute for the transaction-account balance, and the arrangement must be reviewed to determine whether the savings account should be considered to be a transaction account under section 204.2(e)(5).

Question 3: Do transfers from a savings account to another deposit at the institution count toward the six-transfer limit? Does it matter what type of account the funds are transferred to — for example, a demand deposit account or an individual retirement account? Does it matter whether the transfers are for a specific amount and occur on the same day each month — for example, to pay rent?

Transfers from a savings account to another deposit account at the institution would count toward the six-transfer limit if they were made by telephone or by any other means listed in section 204.2(d)(2), regardless of whether the transfers are made on a particular day each month or whether the amount of the transfer varies or is constant from month to month and regardless of the type of account the funds are transferred to.

Question 4: Verify that transactions are correctly categorized according to the following list:

- *Three-transaction limit.* Point-of-sale transactions with either ATM or credit card company debit cards and withdrawals payable to third parties initiated by checks or drafts.

- *Six-transaction limit.* Preauthorized transfers through ACH or EFT; automatic transfers for overdraft protection; telephone, fax, and computer transactions to transfer funds to another account at the same institution; transfers between a parent's account and a child's account; and withdrawals initiated by telephone where the proceeds are paid to third parties.

- *Unlimited.* Transfers to pay loans at the same institution; withdrawals made (1) in person, (2) at an ATM, (3) by messenger, or (4) by mail (via a check sent to the depositor); telephone withdrawals where the withdrawn funds are mailed to the account holder; and transfers between accounts of the depositor at the same institution initiated (1) in person, (2) by mail, (3) by ATM, or (4) by messenger.

The transfers listed under the three-transfer limit are subject to that limit. The transfers listed under the six-transfer limit are generally subject to that limit, and the transactions listed in the unlimited-transfer category generally are not subject to specific transfer limits. However, overdraft-protection arrangements and transfers to pay loans at the same institution could result in a savings account being classified as a transaction account under section 204.2(e)(5). STAFF OP. of July 13, 1992. *Authority: 12 CFR 204.2(d)(2) and (e)(5).*

Time Deposits

Early Withdrawal — Greater-Than-Required Penalty

A bank is free to impose a greater penalty for the withdrawal of time deposits before maturity than that prescribed by Regulation D, as long as the actual penalty is clearly brought to the attention of the depositor on creation of the deposit agreement. STAFF OP. of January 27, 1975. *Authority: 12 CFR 204.2(c).*

Funds Held in Escrow

An escrow account for tax and insurance premiums in which the entire beneficial interest is held by one or more individual mortgagees who qualify in their own right to hold a NOW account or a personal time deposit may qualify as such an account or deposit. STAFF OP. of May I, 1975. *Authority: 12 CFR 204.2(f) and 204.130.*

Early Withdrawal — Transfer of Bank Assets and Liabilities

If a member bank transfers the assets and liabilities (including its certificates of deposit) of one of its branches to a newly chartered banking institution, the transfer of deposits does not constitute an early withdrawal of time deposit funds, and no early withdrawal penalty should be imposed so long as new certificates are issued on the same terms and conditions as the original certificates (that is, at the same rate of interest and maturity). It is appropriate, however, for the member bank to inform the depositors affected that they are under no obligation to exchange their certificates for newly issued instruments. In addition, the depositors should be notified that the early withdrawal penalty would be applied if they were to redeem their deposits before maturity, since a new certificate would represent only a change in the obligor of the instrument, and not a change in any of the terms, including the maturity and interest rate payable. STAFF OP. of December 14, 1978. *Authority: 12 CFR 204.2(c)(1).*

Early Withdrawal — Death of Owner

(1) The beneficiary of a Totten trust does not qualify as an "owner" for the purposes of the death exception to the early withdrawal penalty rule. Owner is defined as any individual who at the time of his or her death has either full legal title or beneficial title to all or a portion of the funds and full power of disposition and alienation with respect thereto. Under a Totten trust, the beneficiary acquires legal title to the deposit only on the unequivocal act or declaration of the grantor during his or her lifetime. In the absence of either of these events, the trust is tentative since the grantor has the power to revoke the trust at will, and the beneficiary lacks full power of disposition and alienation with respect to any portion of the funds. STAFF OP. of August 3, 1979. *Authority: 12 CFR 204.2(c).*

(2) State law determines who is owner of time deposit funds, whether named or unnamed. Under the death exception to the early withdrawal penalty rule, a bank should require reasonable assurance that, at the time of his or her death, an individual qualified as an owner of the funds under state law, within the regulatory definition of the term owner. To facilitate determination of ownership when the time deposit is established, the bank may wish to obtain from a depositor a statement concerning whether or not there are other owners. STAFF OP. of December 9, 1977. *Authority: 12 CFR 204.2(c).*

Transferability

A time deposit would not be regarded as transferable if the depository institution added the name of another natural person to the deposit of a natural person in order to create joint ownership, as long as the transaction takes place on the books of the depository institution. STAFF OP. of September 25, 1980. *Authority: 12 CFR 204.2(f)(1)(iv).*

Early Withdrawal — Death of Depositor

A member bank is not required to apply the early withdrawal penalty prescribed in section 204.2 of Regulation D if the time deposit has renewed automatically after the death of the original depositor and title to the time deposit had passed automatically to the depositor's surviving spouse. However, if at the maturity of the deposit, the owner's heir or representative has reinvested the funds in a deposit with a maturity that varies from the maturity of the original deposit, the heir or representative is no longer able to request a penalty-free early withdrawal, because he or she has consciously chosen to change the nature of the decedent's interest, and the new time deposit can therefore no longer be regarded as that of the decedent. STAFF OP. of April 8, 1981. *Authority: 12 CFR 204.2(c).*

Early Withdrawal — Agreement to Pay Before Maturity

A member bank cannot agree in advance to pay a time deposit before maturity. STAFF OP of December 19, 1978. *Authority: 12 CFR 217.4(a) [since revised; now covered by 12 CFR 204.2(c)(1).]*

Early Withdrawal — Zero-Interest-Rate Deposit

Time deposits on which no interest is earned are not inappropriate per se. However, such time deposits should be carefully monitored in view of the opportunity for an institution to avoid or reduce required reserves by classifying funds otherwise subject to the higher reserve requirements of a demand deposit as a zero-interest-rate time deposit. A time deposit on which no interest is paid is subject to the provisions of Regulation D concerning payment before maturity. Since the early withdrawal penalty is a function of the interest rate being paid on the deposit, application of the early withdrawal penalty provides no disincentive to early withdrawal and, in fact, permits the time deposit to function as a demand deposit. Therefore, time deposits on which no interest is paid may not generally be paid before maturity unless one of the mandatory exceptions to the early withdrawal penalty is applicable. STAFF OP. of June 4, 1981. *Authority: 12 CFR 204.2.*

Early Withdrawal — Evasion of Reserve Requirements

The rule, formerly in section 217.4(f) of Regulation Q, requiring that the rate charged by a member bank on a loan to a depositor secured by the depositor's time deposit must be no less than 1 percent in excess of the rate paid on the deposit, was rescinded by the Board effective April 1, 1986. Nevertheless, in certain circumstances, making a loan secured by a time deposit within six days after the date the deposit is opened, rather than assessing a penalty for an early withdrawal, might be considered an evasion of the reserve requirements of Regulation D — for example, if the depositor and the institution agree that the deposit will be withdrawn on the seventh day and used to pay off the loan. STAFF OP. of July 29, 1986.

Early Withdrawal Penalty — Call Provisions

The presence of certain call provisions in a contract for a nonpersonal time deposit with a maturity of 18 months or more would not necessarily require the certificate of deposit to be classified as a nonpersonal time deposit with a maturity of less than 18 months.

Depository institutions propose to issue longer-term deposits that permit a call for redemption by the depository institution a specified period of time after issuance and would provide that redemption would occur on the expiration of a specified time period after notice by the depository institution. For instance, a bank might issue time deposits and provide that it may, on 30 days' notice, call the obligations for redemption on any date after five years from the date of issuance of the deposits. The deposit contract would *not* allow a call by the issuer to be effective any earlier than one and one-half years after the date of issuance of the deposit.

It appears that no withdrawals could be made from the deposit account within the first one and one-half years after the date of the deposit and no withdrawal would occur on less than seven days' notice. Such a deposit is properly classified as a deposit with a maturity of one and one-half years or greater.

The Board assumes that any call by the depository institution results in payment of the entire deposit. Consequently, this opinion does not address the issue of the status of any amounts remaining on deposit after a partial early withdrawal. STAFF OP. of July 23, 1987. *Authority: 12 CFR 204.2(d) and (f)(3).*

Early Withdrawal Penalty — Put Provisions

The presence of certain put provisions in a contract for a nonpersonal time deposit with a maturity of 18 months or more would not necessarily require the deposit to be classified as a nonpersonal time deposit with a maturity of less than 18 months.

Depository institutions propose to issue longer-term deposits that would permit the depositor to put the deposit back to the issuing depository institution (i.e., the depositor could require the depository institution to redeem the deposit) a specified period of time after issuance and would provide that redemption would occur on the expiration of a specified time period after notice by the depositor. For instance, a bank might issue deposits and permit the depositor to present the obligations for redemption, with at least 10 days notice, on any date after five years from the date of issuance of the deposits. Depositors would *not* be allowed to exercise their right to put any earlier than one and one-half years after the date of issuance of the deposit and in no event less than seven days after written notice of the put.

No withdrawals could be made from the deposit account within the first one and one-half years after the date of the deposit, and no withdrawal would occur on less than seven days' notice. Such a deposit is properly classified as a deposit with a maturity of one and one-half years or more. Section 204.2(f)(3) of Regulation D, which describes long-term nonpersonal time deposits, indicates that if no withdrawal is permitted from the deposits during the first one and one-half years, the deposit is properly classified as having a maturity of one and one-half years or more even if early withdrawal of the deposit is permitted after that time.

The Board assumed that any exercise of the right to withdraw occurs after at least seven days' written notice so that such a withdrawal occurs on or after the date 18 months from the date the deposit is opened and results in payment of the entire deposit. Consequently, this opinion does not address the issue of the status of any amounts remaining on deposit after a partial withdrawal. STAFF OP. of August 5. 1988. *Authority: 12 CFR 204.2(d) and (f)(3).*

Reclassification as Transaction Accounts

The question has arisen whether a time deposit may be used to secure a line of credit if the customer could draw on the line of credit other than by appearing at the depository institution, and whether individual draws on a line of credit would count toward the Regulation D transfer limits for savings deposits.

A credit card or other line of credit arrangement secured by a time or savings deposit might not result in the need to reclassify the time or savings deposit as a transaction account in certain cases. The facts of each arrangement must be considered, including the rates of interest charged on the outstanding balances under the lines of credit; the interest earned on the time deposits; the balances ordinarily maintained in the transaction accounts; the activity in the transaction accounts; the frequency with which advances on the lines of credit are satisfied from the savings deposits rather than other funds from the customer, and the extent to which the depository institution suggests, promotes, or otherwise furthers the establishment of the arrangements. If extensions of credit under the arrangement are regularly satisfied from depositor payments rather than from the time or savings deposit, and if the rate of interest charged on the credit extended substantially exceeds the interest earned on the time or savings deposit — e.g., 18 percent vs. 4 percent — then the arrangement generally would not result in a transaction account. Further, individual extensions of credit under the credit line would not count toward the transfer limit on the time or savings deposit as specified in section 204.2(d)(2). STAFF OP. of February 11, 1992. *Authority: 12 CFR 204.2(d)(2) and (e)(5).*

Transaction Accounts

Combined Savings/Checking Statement

Under the account arrangement, a single statement of account is provided for a depositor's savings and checking accounts. Transfers from savings to checking may be made only by teller or through the use of an automated teller machine (ATM). No preauthorized or telephone transfer access to the savings account is provided. Further, a depositor is not permitted to transfer funds from savings to checking solely for the purpose of making a payment to a third party.

The savings account would not be considered a transaction account for reserve maintenance purposes. One aspect of the plan does deserve comment, however. Any advertising, deposit-contract relationships, and statements of account should indicate clearly that two accounts — a savings and a checking account — are involved, to ensure that customers do not think the service provided constitutes a single account. STAFF OP. of October 7, 1980. *Authority: 12 CFR 204.2(e).*

Withdrawals from Savings Account through ATM

Savings accounts should not be regarded as transaction accounts merely because customers of subsidiary banks of a bank holding company may effect cash withdrawals from those accounts through an ATM of either the bank at which they maintain their account or an affiliated bank or because they may effect transfers of funds from a savings account to another account maintained at the same bank by using an ATM or a check-verification terminal of the bank at which they maintain their accounts. Such transactions are similar to effecting a transaction by appearing in person at an institution. STAFF OP. of December 22. 1980. *Authority: 12 CFR 204.2(e).*

Transfers through Institution to Third Parties

A company offers an insurance program to and through credit unions. Under the program, a master policy is issued to the credit union, and the credit union is required by the policy to (1) remit premiums for the portion of insurance that the credit union provides to all members at no cost and (2) remit premiums on behalf of credit union members who have elected to purchase optional additional insurance. The remittance is paid quarterly to the company after the credit union is furnished with a printout listing the total due from the credit union and each of its members participating in the optional insurance. The credit union apparently is authorized by each member to deduct the optional insurance premium from the member's share account. The credit union then transfers each such payment to its general account and then draws a single credit union draft to cover the total amount due from the credit union under the group plan and from the members under the optional plan.

It appears that the deductions from the accounts would be "preauthorized transfers" as that term is used in section 204.2(e)(6). Consequently, such a transfer would be counted toward the maximum of three transfers per month permitted from a savings deposit or account before it will be considered a transaction account. However, if no more than three transfers, including transfer from the account, can be made during any calendar month or statement cycle of at least four weeks, the account would not be considered a transaction account for purposes of Regulation D and would not be subject to Federal Reserve requirements.

The last sentence of section 204.2(e)(6) of Regulation D states that an account is not a transaction account "by virtue of an arrangement that "permits withdrawals for the purpose of repaying loans and associated expenses at the same depository institution (as originator or servicer)." This exemption, however, does not apply to transfers to third parties on behalf of depositors or account holders, such as in the arrangement above. STAFF OP. of June 22, 1981. *Authority: 12 CFR 204.2(e)(⬜).*

Savings Account Allowing Transfers to Agent Institutions

A state-chartered, state-insured savings and loan association proposes a savings account in which the depositor may make withdrawals by personal transactions at the office of the association or by specific written request. The depositor also may appoint an agent, or grant a power of attorney to another person or institution authorizing the agent to make withdrawals on the depositor's behalf. Depositors would maintain accounts at other depository institutions and name these institutions as agents with respect to the accounts maintained at the institution proposing the plan, thus allowing the agent to make transfers between the accounts at the various institutions. These arrangements would be considered a preauthorized transfer within the meaning of section 204.2(e)(6) of Regulation D because the agent institution in the proposal would represent the third party to whom payment from the depositor's account is made. STAFF OP. of December 23, 1981. *Authority: 12 CFR 204.2(e)(⬚).*

Transfers through ATMs, RSUs, and CVTs

An account is not a transaction account by virtue of permitting transfers to other accounts of the depositor at the same institution through an ATM or remote service unit (RSU). Whether an ATM or RSU is owned by the bank where the account is maintained does not affect these rules. Expanding the number of ATMs or RSUs at which such transactions can be effected does not result in giving customers the degree of convenience normally associated with transactions accounts. Therefore, permitting account holders to transfer funds from a savings account to another account at the same bank through an ATM or check verification terminal (CVT) of an affiliated bank would not result in the savings account being regarded as a transaction account for purposes of Regulation D. STAFF OP. of December 24, 1981. *Authority: 12 CFR 204.2(e)(4).*

Transfers Exempt from Regulation E

Question 3-10 of the official staff commentary on Regulation E states that automatic transfers of funds from deposit accounts to pay premiums on group life insurance available only through the depository institution are bona fide intra-institutional transfers that are exempt from the provisions of Regulation E. Because Regulations D and E serve different purposes, the fact that certain transfers are exempt from Regulation E does not mean that accounts that permit such transfers are exempt from Regulation D. Although the transaction does not require application of the consumer protections of Regulation E, the nature of the transaction as a third-party payment is specifically the type of transfer that, when permitted through a deposit account, is intended to subject such an account to the reserve requirements of Regulation D. STAFF OP. of May 14, 1982. *Authority: 12 CFR 204.2(e).*

CD with Line of Credit

The question has arisen whether a certificate of deposit that is tied to a line of credit equal in amount to the certificate of deposit is a transaction account if the customer may access the line of credit only by appearing in person at the bank. Because the customer may gain access to the line of credit only by appearing in person at the bank, the certificate of deposit associated with this line of credit would not be a transaction account. STAFF OP. of July 27, 1983. *Authority: 12 CFR 204.2(e)(1)(0 ii).*

Withdrawals through ATMs; Transfers through ATM or POS Terminal

Generally, transfers by a customer at an ATM from one of the customer's accounts to another at the same depository institution, and ATM withdrawals paid directly to the customer are not counted toward the permissible number of transfers and withdrawals from ordinary savings accounts or money market deposit accounts. It does not matter whether the depository institution owns the ATM, has exclusive use of it, or shares the ATM owned by another entity. However, all transactions involving a transfer of funds from a customer's account to the account of a third party, whether through an ATM or a point-of-sale (POS) terminal, count toward the transfer limit. It is the character of the underlying transfer (that is, whether the payment initiated by the customer is made directly to the customer or the customer's account rather than to a third party or third party's account) that determines whether the transfer counts in distinguishing a savings and a transaction account. STAFF OP. of July 29, 1986. *Authority: 12 CFR 204.2(d)(2).*

ATM Card as Debit Card — POS Transactions

A bank offers an ATM access card to its consumer customers to use on a network of ATMs to perform banking transactions affecting their accounts. The card is available to any holder of any consumer deposit account to which there is ATM access, which includes holders of savings, money market deposit, checking, and NOW accounts.

The bank is negotiating a POS agreement with an oil company to permit holders of transaction accounts to purchase the oil company's products and services by using ATM cards as debit cards at the oil company's service stations. Only checking and NOW account customers will be authorized to use the ATM card in this manner, and only these transaction accounts will be debited. The computer that will operate the system will be programmed to permit debit card transactions only on checking or NOW accounts, and not on savings or money market deposit accounts.

A potential problem arises when the computer system is down and holders of ATM cards linked to savings accounts and money market deposit accounts attempt to obtain services from the oil company by using their ATM cards as debit cards. The back-up authorization system, the service station operator, and the POS terminal will be unable to identify and reject a purchase transaction involving an ATM card issued on a savings or money market deposit account because the card is not electronically distinguishable from the ATM cards issued on checking or NOW accounts. If a savings account customer, even though previously instructed not to use an ATM card to make service station purchases, attempts to do so while the authorization system is operating off-line, a circumstance which is expected to be exceedingly rare, a POS transaction will result. The bank will implement an ex post monitoring procedure, designed to meet the requirements of section 204.2(d)(2), footnote 5, of Regulation D, to identify such transactions. Any unauthorized transaction will be identified, and the bank will warn the customer that the account agreement has been violated and that, if further unauthorized transactions occur, the ATM card will be canceled.

In this particular case, although Regulation D generally prohibits withdrawals from a savings deposit made by a debit card, the bank need not reclassify the savings accounts as transaction accounts because it is expected that unauthorized transactions will be rare, and appropriate monitoring procedures will be in place. However, if the bank does not make reasonable good faith efforts to monitor unauthorized transactions and prevent future unauthorized transactions, reclassification of the savings accounts and MMDAs will be required. STAFF OP. of July 29, 1986. *Authority: 12 CFR 204.2(d)(1) and (2).*

Bona Fide Cash Management

A depository institution may not net overdrafts in demand deposits or other transaction accounts against demand deposits or other transaction accounts with positive balances when calculating its aggregate transaction accounts for reserve purposes. Overdrafts are properly reflected on the books of the institution as assets in the form of extensions of credit. If overdrafts in accounts could be treated as negative balances and netted against positive balances in other accounts, depository institutions would under-report and under-reserve their aggregate transaction accounts. However, bona fide cash-management arrangements are expected. The Board has been asked whether agreements for bona fide cash-management arrangements may be either oral or written and whether the arrangements may be used with intra-company accounts and with accounts held by affiliated companies.

Depository institutions and their customers have flexibility in establishing multiple accounts for cash-management purposes when funds could be placed in one account. Although such an arrangement does not necessarily require a prior written agreement, a written agreement would help a depository institution establish that a particular arrangement comes within that exception.

Generally, a bona fide cash-management arrangement exists and accounts may be netted for reserve purposes when the depository institution and the customer in effect treat the accounts as a single account and the institution has an unrestricted right to offset against one account to cover overdrafts in another account. Generally, the exception applies only to the related accounts of one depositor or to accounts of related depositors (such as cosigners, family members, and interdependent entities) when all the depositors have unfettered use of the funds in all accounts, the multiple accounts are established for the customers' convenience, and there is no legal impediment to the commingling of funds in the accounts. STAFF OP. of August 14, 1986. *Authority: 12 CFR 204.❑ (e).*

Automatic Transfers of Savings

If a member bank owns or uses ATMs that cannot be readily modified to permit direct withdrawals from a savings deposit subject to automatic transfers, an ATM may be used to initiate a withdrawal from a checking account that would result in an automatic transfer from the savings deposit account. The bank must, however, provide alternate means of access to savings deposit accounts subject to automatic transfer service (ATS), such as effecting a withdrawal by personal appearance at the bank or by telephone. Withdrawal slips for a savings account subject to automatic transfer do not have to be made available in the bank lobby, and a bank may require depositors to request the slips from bank personnel. However, customers should be notified of this fact when the automatic transfer service is authorized.

Member banks are permitted to offer ATS to trusteeships, guardianships, and other personal accounts if the entire beneficial interest in the funds on deposit is held by one or more individuals. The use of a single monthly statement for accounts involved in an ATS plan is permissible; however, the statement should clearly reflect the distinct nature of the two accounts, possibly indicating the beginning and ending balances in each account as well as each withdrawal and transfer effected by the depositor. STAFF OP. of October 27, 1978. *Authority: 12 CFR 204.2(e).*

Transfers from Savings to Cover NOW Overdrafts

An overdraft protection plan that involves transfers from a savings account to cover overdrafts in a NOW account would not cause the account to be regarded as a transaction account unless more than three transfers can be effected by telephone or through preauthorized arrangement in one calendar month or one monthly billing cycle. STAFF OP. of September 24, 1980. *Authority: 12 CFR 204.2(0)(0) and 204.2(e).*

Point-of-Sale Terminals

A company is considering offering service that will allow a customer to make purchases at a POS location with a debit card (with direct credit to the merchant's account) or with scrip obtained at the POS terminal (with an immediate debit to the customer's account and credit to the merchant's account). The customer also would have the option of exchanging the scrip for cash from that merchant rather than using the scrip to make a purchase from that merchant. Under either arrangement, the customer is in effect making a third-party payment to the merchant. Several questions were raised about the effect of alternative features of the service on the reserve treatment of accounts subject to POS access.

Briefly, allowing access to an ordinary savings account through either the scrip arrangement or the direct debit card transfer arrangement would cause that account to be classified as a transaction account. However, both arrangements can be used with a MMDA, and the account would not be a transaction account unless the customer is permitted or authorized to make more than three such transactions per month.

Under section 202.2(d)(2)(i) of Regulation D, a savings deposit is not considered a transaction account, even though the depositor is permitted to make up to three withdrawals per month for the purpose of moving funds to another account of the depositor or making payments to third parties, as long as none of the withdrawals or transfers may be made by check, draft, or similar order, including debit card. The definition of "savings deposit" also includes an MMDA from which the depositor is permitted to make up to six withdrawals per month for the purpose of moving funds to another account of the depositor or making payments to third parties; and no more than three of these six transfers may be by check, draft, debit card, or similar order made by the depositor and payable to third parties (204.2(d)(2)(ii)). However, such an account will not meet this definition if the customer is authorized or permitted to make more than six withdrawals or transfers or three third-party payment orders per month. In that case, the account would be considered a transaction account subject to the higher reserves applicable to such accounts (204.2(e)(2)). Consequently, MMDAs used with either the scrip arrangement or the debit card arrangement would not be regarded as transaction accounts so long as access by debit card is limited to an aggregate of six withdrawals and transfers per month, with no more than three of the withdrawals or transfers being by check or debit card, including debit card transactions at POS terminals.

Regulation D bases its distinctions between accounts on whether the depositor, by agreement or practice of the depository institution, *i* *er* *itted or authori* ed to make such withdrawals or transfers and not on whether the withdrawals or transfers are actually made. Thus, an institution could offer MMDAs with and without POS access. Generally, if any of the depositors with such access are permitted or authorized to exceed the three-per-month limitation, then the board would consider any account permitting or authorizing such access a transaction account. Footnotes 5 and 6 of Regulation D provide for such monitoring on an ex post basis and for exceptions to the rule for occasional excess transfers. STAFF OP. of August 11, 1986. *Authority: 12 CFR 204.2(d)(2)(i) and (ii)* *and 204.2(e).*

Transfers from MMDA to Cover Line of Credit

The Board has been asked about the proper treatment of a proposed arrangement consisting of an account intended to qualify as a MMDA, a demand deposit account, and a line of credit to cover overdrafts in the demand deposit account. Checks drawn on the demand deposit account in excess of the balance would be paid from loan proceeds transferred to the account, and the bank would note a drawing on the line of credit. Once a week, funds from the MMDA would be transferred to cover outstanding balances on the line of credit. The interest rate imposed on drawings on the line of credit would be equal to that paid on the MMDA, adjusted to account for the effect of reserves. The MMDA would secure the line of credit, which would be limited to the amount deposited in the MMDA. If, at the end of a day, there are balances in the demand deposit account in excess of a specified minimum, the excess would be used to pay any amount owed on the line of credit and any excess would be transferred into the MMDA.

Under section 204.2(e)(5) of Regulation D, an account maintained in connection with an arrangement that permits a depositor to obtain credit directly or indirectly through the drawing of checks is a transaction account. The proposed arrangement falls under that section; therefore, the MMDA would be a transaction account subject to a 12 percent reserve requirement because (1) the MMDA would regularly be used to repay the line of credit; (2) interest on the line of credit would be tied to the interest rate on the MMDA; (3) the line of credit would be secured by the MMDA; and (4) drawings on the line of credit would result from overdrafts in a demand deposit account on which the checks were drawn.

The Board has previously stated that a transfer out of an MMDA to repay an extension of credit by a depository institution, where the extension of credit was previously made to cover an overdraft on that MMDA, does not result in a separate transfer countable against the MMDA transfer limits. In that case, the transfer giving rise to the overdraft counted as one third-party transfer, and the repayment of the overdraft constituted the repayment of a loan by the depository institution and not a third-party transfer. That opinion did not apply to a prearranged plan linking an MMDA to a line of credit in a situation that would permit the customer to exceed the MMDA transfer limits by writing checks against the line of credit. STAFF OP. of October 3, 1989. *Authority: 12 CFR 204.2(e)(5)▯ 204.2(d)(2)(ii)▯ and 204.5(e).*

Combined MMDA and Demand Deposit

Several depository institutions were offering an account arrangement to some customers that combined a MMDA with a demand deposit. Typically, the depository institution allowed a customer to create overdrafts in a demand deposit during the week and then pay off the aggregate overdraft at the end of the week with one transfer from the MMDA. The rate of interest paid on the money market deposit account equals the rate of interest charged on the overdraft line of credit, and the number of transfers from the MMDA to cover the overdrafts would never exceed the six-per-month limit that applies to automatic interaccount transfers. Thus, the depository institution considered the demand account balance as zero when it calculated its transaction accounts and included the balance in the MMDA in its time deposits when filing Form FR 2900.

Section 204.2(e)(5) was added to Regulation D because arrangements involving time deposits and credit lines are effective substitutes for transaction accounts and provide the opportunity to avoid transaction-account reserve requirements. This section clearly covers this type of account arrangement. Therefore, the arrangement and the way the depository institutions reported the deposits constitute violations of Regulation D. STAFF OP. of July 1, 1991. *Authority: 12 CFR 204.2(e)(5).*

Transfers from Demand Accounts for Investment Purposes

A bank proposes to provide a service to customers that would involve coordination among the bank, its customers, and an independent trust company organized under state law. Each customer would authorize the bank to transfer the amount above a predetermined level in its demand account to a pooled demand account maintained by the trust company at the bank. At the direction of the customer, the trust company would then place those funds in a variety of investments, including a money market account at the bank and professionally managed money funds. The customer would deal directly with the trust company on all issues involving the invested funds. The bank would not be involved with the funds other than to facilitate the transfer of funds between accounts as directed by the customer or the trust company. Demand-account overdrafts are not anticipated, but if an overdraft did occur, the bank would inform the trust company, which would transfer funds to the customer's account to cover the overdraft.

This trust arrangement is, in effect, substantially similar to an arrangement described in interpretation 12 CFR 204.134, in which the Board indicated that the arrangement in which customers maintain checking accounts and have excess funds from those accounts swept into commingled time deposits was an arrangement that:

> Substitutes time deposit balances for transaction accounts balances with no practical restrictions on the depositors' access to their funds,

and serves no business purpose other than to allow the payment of higher interest through the avoidance of reserve requirements. As the time deposits may be used to provide funds indirectly for the purposes of making payments or transfers to third persons, the Board has determined that the time deposits should be considered to be transaction accounts for purposes of Regulation D.

The Board believes that this interpretation applies to the proposed trust arrangement. STAFF OP. of July 16, 1992. *Authority: 12 CFR 204.2(d)(2)▯ 204.2(e)▯ and 204.1▯ 4.*

Laws

12 USC 1832, Consumer Checking Account Equity Act

12 USC 461, Reserve Requirements

Regulations

12 CFR 204, Reserve Requirements of Depository Institutions

Interest on Deposits

Background and Summary

Regulation Q prohibits the payment of interest on demand deposits held by banks that are members of the Federal Reserve System and, generally, by U.S. branches and agencies of foreign banks with worldwide consolidated assets greater than $1 billion. It does not apply to deposits payable only at an office of a member bank or a foreign bank located outside the states of the United States and the District of Columbia. Interest is any payment made to a depositor as compensation for the use of deposit funds. Payment of interest does not include a bank's absorption of its normal banking expenses. Services such as free checking accounts, loans at reduced rates, and free money orders are examples of absorbed fees that are not considered payment of interest.

Regulation Q's definition of a *demand deposit* is merely a cross-reference to that in Regulation D. Demand deposits, subject to the prohibition against the payment of interest, do not include NOW accounts, automatic transfer service (ATS) accounts, ordinary savings deposits, or money market deposit accounts.

All provisions relating to disclosures and the advertisement of deposit accounts were deleted from Regulation Q effective June 21, 1993. Disclosure and advertising are now governed by Regulation DD, Truth in Savings.

Federal Reserve Board Staff Opinions Interpreting Regulation Q

The staff opinions below address Regulation Q, Interest on Deposits. They provide guidance for compliance with Regulation Q.

Indirect Payment of Interest

Any actual payment or credit to or for the account of a depositor, as distinguished from a bank's not charging for normal banking services, is regarded as an indirect payment of interest. The Federal Reserve Board has considered the offering of the following services without charge in exchange for municipal funds being deposited with member banks, not to be payment of interest:

- Loans at preferential interest rates.
- Armored car service.
- Short-term overdraft privileges.
- Full endorsement stamps.
- Rubber stamps.
- Printed checks.
- Bonded safekeeping of municipality's securities.
- Safe deposit box and night depository facilities.
- Processing of shipping and insurance in connection with transfers on collections of municipal bonds or bond coupons.
- Preparation of reports required of the bank by the municipality.
- Service as paying agent on bonds.
- Maintenance of a permanent record of all checks and deposits.

These items are regarded as ordinary banking services for which the bank simply agrees not to impose a charge.

A bank's agreement to assume the responsibility for the operation of a state's warrant-processing and -reconciliation system, in exchange for the state's deposits, does not constitute payment of interest if bank costs resulting from provision of its computer facilities, including use of bank personnel, can be characterized as those relating to ordinary banking business. STAFF OP. of January 3, 1974. *Authority: 12 CFR 217.2( ) (re ed no 12 CFR 217.2(d)).*

Absorption or Reduction of Charges vs. Rebate

As a general rule, absorption or reduction of charges for banking services would not constitute the payment of interest, since the bank does not actually pay funds to the depositor, although the customer does benefit from the charges absorbed. This should be distinguished, however, from instances in which a rebate is actually paid to the customer based on a deposit balance maintained at the bank. In certain circumstances, such a practice could be viewed as a payment of interest for purposes of Regulation Q. STAFF OP. of October 27, 1978. *Authority: 12 CFR 217.2( ) (re ed no 12 CFR 217.2(d)).*

Services Provided by Subsidiaries of Bank Customers

The Board was asked whether payments by a member bank to a third-party vendor (the service provider) for services provided to an escrow company that is a demand-deposit customer of the member bank would be considered indirect payment of interest on a demand deposit.

The service provider, a wholly owned subsidiary of the escrow company, provides services only to the escrow company. Under a contract between the escrow company and the service provider, fees are paid for accounting and data processing services that the service provider renders to the escrow company to account for funds that have been deposited in the demand deposit account at the member bank. Generally, the charges for services performed by the service provider are exactly the same as the value of the earnings credits available to the escrow company.

Under section 217.2(d) of Regulation Q, "[a] member bank's absorption of expenses incident to providing a normal banking function or its forbearance from charging a fee in connection with such a service is not considered a payment of interest." A member bank may provide a "normal banking function" through a third party without violating Regulation Q. A bank that does not have, or chooses not to allocate, the resources to directly provide services by bank employees may provide them under contract with a third-party vendor. However, the vendor may provide those services only if there is no payment "to or for the account" of the bank customers and if the provision of those services by a third-party vendor is the functional equivalent of provision directly by the bank. For example, a member bank may contract with a corporation to provide banking services to the bank for the benefit of customers of the bank. In this case, the provision of the services would be controlled by the bank and the service provider would merely be a substitute for the bank. The customer could receive an earnings credit based on the average daily balance it maintains in a demand deposit account to be applied against the costs of the services. In this example, the bank makes no payment "to or for the account" of the customer. The payments by the bank to the vendor are solely based on the contract between the bank and the vendor. Accordingly, the payments made by the bank to the vendor would not constitute interest to the customer.

However, in this case the payment provided by the bank to the service provider constitutes the payment of interest under Regulation Q. The payments are made to the service provider, a wholly owned subsidiary of the escrow company, a customer of the bank, and thus the payments for those services would be considered payments "to or for the account" of the escrow company. STAFF OPs. of September 28, 1993, and November 24, 1993. Authority: 12 CFR 217.2(d) and 217.0.

Interest on Demand Deposits

Earnings Credits to Reduce Loan Charges

A bank is considering an arrangement with certain corporate depositors in which it would make loans to the depositors at a low rate of interest. The rate would be based on earnings credits attributed to compensating balances that the customers would maintain in demand accounts or savings accounts, or both.

The bank would not lend all the money directly but would arrange with other banks to lend varying amounts to the corporate customers at favorable interest rates. Using an agreed-on formula, the bank would remit a portion of the amount it allows customers as earnings credits to the other lending banks. Consequently, the other lending banks would share in the benefits from the compensating balances. Although the borrowers generally would not be involved in setting up the transactions with the participating banks, there may be times when the borrowers would work directly with them.

Section 217.2(d) of Regulation Q specifically allows a member bank to forbear from charging a fee if a customer maintains a compensating balance in a demand deposit account. Therefore, the bank may provide its customers loans at a reduced rate of interest based on compensating balances in a demand deposit account. However, the bank may not otherwise convert accrued earnings credits into payments to the customer. If the bank makes payments directly to other depository institutions on the basis of balances maintained by its customers in order to induce those depository institutions to provide loans to its customers at favorable rates, the bank is making payments "to or for the account" of its depositors. Thus, the arrangement appears to be a means to evade the prohibitions against the payment of interest on demand deposits.

In the transactions contemplated, if the customers maintain funds in any demand deposit accounts that are used in determining the earnings credits, the bank would be prohibited from crediting another depository institution with any earnings credits earned by the customers regardless of whether a majority of the compensating balances are maintained in demand deposits or whether a majority are maintained in interest-bearing accounts. However, a customer would be free to remit interest earned from an interest-bearing account, such as a time deposit, to a third party. STAFF OP. of June 28, 1988. Authority: FRA 19(0)(12); 0 C(0) 1a(; 12 CFR 21(0).2(d).

Lower Loan Charges Based on Balances

Banks controlled by a bank holding company want to offer loans to customers maintaining large demand deposit balances. A portion of these loans would be made at a favorable rate. The loan proceeds would be used to purchase commercial paper, Treasury bills, or other instruments, and these investment instruments would be pledged as security for the loans. Before extending credit, each bank would review the past demand-account transactions to determine the amount it would be willing to lend based on the average balance in each demand account and to determine the amount of an earnings credit it would allow each demand account. For every dollar that the average is above the amount necessary to meet the reserve requirement and to meet the compensating balance required to pay the service charges associated with each account, the bank would extend new credit at a favorable rate to the customer. The balance of the new funds lent would be lent at a market rate of interest.

These transactions would not result in the payment of interest on demand accounts. There are no payments to or for the accounts of the depositors. Rather, the banks would be absorbing expenses incident to providing a normal banking function or forbearing from charging a fee in connection with the provision of a normal banking service. The earning credits attributable to any demand deposit account would not be used to offset interest charges already incurred by the depositors. Use of earnings credits for purposes other than absorbing current expenses incident to providing a normal banking function would result in payments to or for the accounts of the depositors on demand deposit accounts in violation of Regulation Q. STAFF OP. of June 28, 1988. *Authority:* 12 CFR 217.3 and 217.2(d).

Laws
> 12 USC 371a, Federal Reserve Act

Regulations
> 12 CFR 217, Prohibition against the Payment of Interest on Demand
> Deposits

Expedited Funds Availability

Background and Summary

The Expedited Funds Availability Act (EFA Act) was enacted in August 1987 and became effective in September 1988. The Check Clearing for the 21st Century Act (Check 21) was enacted October 28, 2003, with an effective date of October 28, 2004. Availability of Funds and Collection of Checks – Regulation CC (12 CFR 229), issued by the Board of Governors of the Federal Reserve System (Board), implements the EFA in subparts A through C and Check 21 in subpart D. Regulation CC sets forth the requirements that depository institutions make funds deposited into transaction accounts available according to specified time schedules and that they disclose their funds availability policies to their customers. The regulation also establishes rules designed to speed the collection and return of unpaid checks. The Check 21 section of the regulation describes requirements that affect banks that create or receive substitute checks, including consumer disclosures and expedited recredit procedures.

Availability of Funds and Disclosure of Funds Availability Policies

Next-Day Availability — 12 CFR 229.10

Cash, electronic payments, and certain check deposits generally must be made available for withdrawal the business day after the banking day on which they were received. Among the covered check deposits are cashier's, certified, and teller's checks, government checks (including U.S. Treasury checks, U.S. Postal Service money orders, state and local government checks, checks drawn on Federal Reserve or Federal Home Loan banks), and certain "on us" checks (checks drawn on the same bank or a branch thereof).

$100 Rule

12 CFR 229.10(c)(1)(vii) of the regulation contains a special $100 rule for check deposits not subject to next-day availability. Under the rule, the depository bank must make available for withdrawal the lesser of $100 or the aggregate amount deposited to all accounts, including individual and joint accounts, held by the same customer on any one banking day. The $100 rule does not apply to deposits received at nonproprietary ATMs.

Availability Schedule — 12 CFR 229.12

Under this schedule, local check deposits must be made available no later than the second business day following the banking day of deposit. Deposits of nonlocal checks must be made available no later than the fifth business day following the banking day of deposit. Funds, including cash and all checks, deposited at nonproprietary ATMs must be made available no later than the fifth business day following the banking day on which the funds were deposited.

Cash Withdrawals

Special rules apply to cash withdrawals from local and nonlocal check deposits. While 12 CFR 229.12 (d) allows the depository bank to extend the availability schedule for cash or similar withdrawals by one day, the customer must still be allowed to withdraw the first $100 of any check deposit not subject to next-day availability on the business day following the day of deposit. In addition to the first $100, a customer must also be allowed to withdraw $400 of the deposited funds (or the maximum amount that can be withdrawn from an ATM, but not more than $400) no later than 5 p.m. on the day funds become available for check withdrawals. The remainder of deposited funds would be available for cash withdrawal on the following business day.

Permanent Funds Availability Schedules — Figure A

Illustrates availability of different types of checks deposited the *same* day, under the schedules.

Monday (Day 0)	Tuesday (Day 1)	Wednesday (Day 2)	Thursday (Day 3)	Friday (Day 4)	Monday (Day 5)	Tuesday (Day 6)	Wednesday (Day 7)	Thursday (Day 8)

Legend:
- ○ Deposit
- □ Cash
- △ Check

Local — Deposit $1,000
- Tuesday (Day 1): Check 1 $100; Cash 1 $100
- Wednesday (Day 2): Check 2 $900; Cash 4 $400
- Thursday (Day 3): Cash 5 $500

Nonlocal — Deposit $1,000
- Tuesday (Day 1): Check 1 $100; Cash 1 $100
- Monday (Day 5): Check 3 $900; Cash 4 $400
- Tuesday (Day 6): Cash 5 $500

[1] The first $100 of a day's deposit must be made available for either cash withdrawal or check writing purposes at the start of the next business day (229.10(c)(1)(vii)).

[2] Local checks must be made available for check writing purposes by the second business day following deposit (229.12(b)).

[3] Nonlocal checks must be made available for check writing purposes by the fifth business day following deposit (229.12(c)).

[4] $400 of the local deposit must be made available for cash withdrawal no later than 5:00 p.m. on the day specified in the schedule. This is in addition to the $100 that must be made available on the business day following deposit (229.12(d)).

[5] The remainder of the deposit must be made available for cash withdrawal at the start of business the following day (229.12(d)).

Permanent Funds Availability Schedules — Figure B

Illustrates availability of different types of checks deposited on *separate* days, under the schedules.

Monday (Day 0)	Tuesday (Day 1)	Wednesday (Day 2)	Thursday (Day 3)	Friday (Day 4)	Monday (Day 5)	Tuesday (Day 6)	Wednesday (Day 7)	Thursday (Day 8)

Local

$1,000 Deposit

Local: Triangle 1 $100 (Friday), Triangle 2 $900 (Monday)

Cash Withdrawal 1 $100 (Friday)

Cash Withdrawal 4 $400 (Monday), Cash Withdrawal 5 $1,400 (Tuesday)

Nonlocal

$1,000 Deposit

Cash Withdrawal 1 $100 (Tuesday)

Check Writing 1 $100 (Tuesday), Check Writing 3 $900 (Monday)

Legend:
- ◯ Deposit
- ▭ Cash Withdrawals
- △ Check Writing

---

[1] The first $100 of a day's deposit must be made available for either cash withdrawal or check writing purposes at the start of the next business day (229.10(c)(1)(vii)).

[2] Local checks must be made available for check writing purposes by the second business day following deposit (229.12(b)).

[3] Nonlocal checks must be made available for check writing purposes by the fifth business day following deposit (229.12(c)).

[4] $400 of the local deposit must be made available for cash withdrawal no later than 5:00 p.m. on the day specified in the schedule. This is in addition to the $100 that must be made available on the business day following deposit (229.12(d)).

[5] The remainder of the deposit must be made available for cash withdrawal at the start of business the following day (229.12(d)).

Exceptions — 12 CFR 229.13

The regulation provides six exceptions that allow banks to exceed the maximum hold periods in the availability schedules. The regulation regards the exceptions as "safeguards" to the maximum availability time frames because they are intended to offer the institution a means of reducing risk based on the size of the deposit, past performance of the depositor, lack of depositor performance history, or belief that the deposit may not be collectible. These exceptions include:

- New accounts;
- Deposits that exceed $5,000 on any one day;
- Checks that have been returned unpaid and are being redeposited;
- Deposits to accounts that have been repeatedly overdrawn;
- Checks that the bank has reasonable cause to believe are uncollectible; and
- Emergency conditions.

Note: Sections 229.10(c) and 229.12 apply to new account exception but not the other exceptions.

New Accounts Exception

An account is considered a "new account" under 12 CFR 229.13(a) for the first 30 days after it is established. An account is not considered "new" if each customer on the account had another established account at the bank for at least 30 calendar days. The new account exception applies only during the 30-day period, beginning on the date the account is established. Certain types of deposits (cash and electronic deposits) made to a new account are not covered by this exception.

Large Deposit Exception (Deposits Exceeding $5,000)

Under 12 CFR 229.13(b), the large deposit exception, a depository bank may extend hold schedules when deposits other than cash or electronic payments exceed $5,000 on any one day. A hold may be applied to the amount that exceeds $5,000. To apply the rule, the depository bank may aggregate deposits made to multiple accounts held by the same customer, even if the customer is not the sole owner of the accounts.

Redeposited Check Exception

Under 12 CFR 229.13(c), the depository bank may delay the availability of funds from a check if the check had previously been deposited and returned unpaid. This exception does not apply to checks that were previously returned unpaid because of a missing endorsement or because the check was postdated when presented.

Repeated Overdraft Exception

12 CFR 229.13(d), provides that if a customer's account, or accounts, have been repeatedly overdrawn during the preceding six months, the bank may delay the availability of funds from checks.

Exception for Doubting a Check's Collectibility

This exception, in 12 CFR 229.13(e), may be applied to all checks. To trigger this exception, the depository institution must have "reasonable cause" to doubt that the check is collectible and must disclose the basis for the extended hold to the customer. For example, reasonable cause may include communication with the paying bank indicating that:

* A stop payment has been placed on the check;

* The drawer's account has insufficient funds; or

* The check will be returned unpaid.

Overdraft and Returned Check Fees

Under 12 CFR 229.13(e)(2), if a depository bank invokes the "reasonable cause" exception and does not inform the customer in writing at the time of the deposit, the bank may not charge the customer any overdraft or returned-check fees resulting from the hold if:

* The deposited check is paid by the paying bank; and

- The overdraft or returned check would not have occurred had the depository bank not imposed the hold.

However, the depository bank may assess overdraft or returned-check fees if, when notifying the customer that the check is held, the notice states that the customer may be entitled to a refund of any overdraft or return-check fees imposed and describes how the customer may obtain such a refund. The bank must then refund the fees upon request.

Emergency Conditions

12 CFR 229.13(f) of the regulation also permits institutions to suspend the availability schedules under emergency conditions.

Notice of Exception

Whenever a bank invokes one of the exceptions (excluding new accounts) to the availability schedules, it must notify the customer in writing in accordance with 12 CFR 229.13(g). Banks may send notices that comply solely with 12 CFR 229.13(g)(1), or may comply with two alternative notice requirements discussed below.

General Notice Requirements

Banks complying with 12 CFR 229.13(g)(1) must send notices which include:

- The customer's account number;

- The date and amount of the deposit;

- The amount of the deposit that will be delayed;

- The reason the exception was invoked; and

- The day the funds will be available for withdrawal (unless unknown, as in an emergency situation).

Payment of Interest — 12 CFR 229.14

General Rule

A depository bank must begin accruing interest on interest-bearing accounts no later than the business day on which it receives provisional credit for the deposited funds. A depository bank typically receives credit on checks within one or two days following deposit. A bank receives credit on a cash deposit, an electronic payment, and a check that is drawn on itself on the day the cash, check, or electronic payment is received. If a nonproprietary ATM is involved, credit is usually received on the day the bank that operates the ATM credits the depository bank for the amount of deposit.

General Disclosure Requirements — 12 CFR 229.15

Form of Disclosure

A bank must disclose its specific availability policy to its customers. The required disclosures must be clear and conspicuous, and must also be in writing under 12 CFR 229.15(a). Disclosures, other than those posted at locations where employees accept consumer deposits, at ATMs or on preprinted deposit slips, must be in a form that the customer may keep. Disclosures must not contain information unrelated to the regulation's requirements. If the disclosures are contained in a document that sets forth other account terms, the disclosure shall be highlighted within the document, for example, by using a separate heading.

Specific Availability Policy Disclosure — 12 CFR 229.16

A bank must provide its customers with a disclosure that describes its funds availability policy. The disclosure must reflect the policy followed by the institution in most cases; however, the institution may impose longer delays on a case-by-case basis or by invoking one of the exceptions in 12 CFR 229.13, provided this is reflected in the disclosure.

Longer Delays on a Case-by-Case Basis

A bank that has a policy of making deposited funds available for withdrawal sooner than required may extend the time when funds are available up to the time periods allowed under the regulation on a case-by-case basis.

Initial Disclosures — 12 CFR 229.17

New Accounts

12 CFR 229.17(a) states that a bank must provide potential customers with the disclosures described in 12 CFR 229.16 before an account is opened.

Additional Disclosure Requirements — 12 CFR 229.18

Deposit Slips

Under 12 CFR 229.18(a), all preprinted deposit slips given to customers must include a notice that deposits may not be available for immediate withdrawal.

Location Where Employees Accept Consumer Deposits

12 CFR 229.18(b) provides that a bank must post, at a conspicuous place at each location where its employees receive deposits to consumer accounts, a notice that sets forth the time periods applicable to the availability of funds deposited.

Automated Teller Machines

Under 12 CFR 229.18(c), a depository bank must post or provide a notice at each ATM location that funds deposited in the ATM may not be available for immediate withdrawal. A depository bank that operates an off-premises ATM from which deposits are removed not more than two times each week, as described in 12 CFR 229.19(a)(4), must disclose at or on the ATM the days in which deposits made at the ATM will be considered received.

Upon Request

12 CFR 229.18(d) states that a bank must provide a copy of its specific availability policy disclosure described in 12 CFR 229.16 to any person who requests it.

Changes in Policy

Thirty days prior to implementing a change in the bank's availability policy, the bank must notify all account holders who are adversely affected by the change. Under 12 CFR 229.18(e), changes that result in faster availability may be disclosed no later than 30 days after implementation.

Miscellaneous — 12 CFR 229.19

When Funds Are Considered Deposited

12 CFR 229.19(a) provides rules that govern when funds are considered, deposited for purposes of part 229's subpart B, Availability of Funds and Disclosure of Funds Availability Policies. The time that funds must be made available for withdrawal is measured from the day the deposit is "received." Funds received at a staffed teller station or ATM is considered deposited when received by the teller or placed in the ATM. Funds mailed to the depository bank are considered deposited on the banking day they are received by the depository bank. The funds are received by the depository bank at the time the mail is delivered to the bank, even if the mail is initially delivered to a mailroom, rather than to the check processing area.

Funds, however, may also be deposited at an unstaffed facility such as a night depository or lock box. Funds deposited at a night depository are considered deposited on the banking day that the deposit is removed, and the contents of the deposit are accessible to the depository bank for processing. For example, some businesses deposit their funds in a locked bag at the night depository late in the evening and return to the bank the following day to open the bag. Other depositors may have an agreement with their bank that the deposit bag must be opened under the dual control of the bank and the depositor. In these cases, the funds are considered deposited when the customer returns to the bank and opens the deposit bag.

Funds deposited in a lock box are considered deposited on the day the deposit is removed from the lock box and are accessible to the depository bank for processing. Corporations typically use a lock box to collect bill payments or other check receipts.

The regulation contains a special rule for off-premise ATMs that are not serviced daily. Funds deposited at these ATMs are considered received on the day they are removed from the ATM, if the ATM is not serviced more than two times each week. This special provision is geared toward banks whose practice is to service remote ATMs infrequently. If a depository bank uses this provision, it must post a notice at the ATM informing depositors that funds deposited at the ATM may not be considered received on the date of deposit.

Funds deposited on a day the depository bank is closed, or after the bank's cut-off hour, may be considered received on the next banking day. Generally, a bank may establish a cut-off hour of 2 p.m. or later for receipt of deposits at its main office or branch offices. A cut-off hour of noon or later may be established for deposits made to ATMs, lock boxes, night depositories, or other off-premises facilities. (As specified in the commentary to 12 CFR 229.19(a), the noon cut-off period relates to the local time of the branch or other location of the depository bank where the account is maintained or the local time of the ATM or off-premise facility.)

Different cut-off hours may be established for different types of deposits. For example, a 2 p.m. cut-off for receipt of check deposits and a later time for receipt of wire transfers is permissible. Location can also play a role in the establishment of cut-off hours. For example, ATM deposits may have a different cut-off hour than over-the-counter deposits, and different teller stations at the same branch may have different cut-off hours. With the exception of the noon cut-off hour for deposits at ATMs and off-premise facilities, no cut-off hour for receipt of deposits can be earlier than 2 p.m.

When Funds Must Be Made Available

12 CFR 229.19(b) discusses funds availability at the start of a business day. Generally, funds must be available for withdrawal by the later of 9 a.m. or the time a depository bank's teller facilities including ATMs are available for customer account withdrawals. (Under certain circumstances, there is a special exception for cash withdrawals–see 12 CFR 229.12(d).) Thus, if a

bank has no ATMs and its branch facilities are available for customer transactions beginning at 10 a.m., funds must be available for withdrawal by 10 a.m. If a bank has 24-hour ATM service, funds must be available by 9 a.m. for ATM withdrawals.

The start of business is determined by the local time where the branch or depository bank holding the account is located. For example, if funds in an account at a West Coast bank are first made available at the start of business on a given day, and a customer attempts to withdraw the funds at an East Coast ATM, the depository bank is not required to make funds available until 9 a.m. Pacific Standard Time (noon Eastern Standard Time).

Employee Training and Compliance

12 CFR 229.19(f) contains the requirements for employee training and compliance. The Expedited Funds Availability Act (EFA Act) requires banks to inform each employee who performs duties subject to the act about its requirements. The EFA Act and Regulation CC also require banks to establish and maintain procedures designed to ensure and monitor employee compliance with such requirements.

Effects of Mergers

12 CFR 229.19(g) explains the effect of a merger transaction. Merged banks may be treated as separate banks for no more than one year after consummation of the merger transaction. A customer of any bank that is a party to the merger transaction and who, as a result, has an established account with the merging bank, may not be treated as a new account holder under the new account exception of 12 CFR 229.13(a). A deposit in any branch of the merged bank is considered deposited in the bank for purposes of the availability schedules in accordance with 12 CFR 220.19(a). This rule affects the status of the combined entity in a number of areas. For example, when:

- An ATM is a "proprietary ATM", or
- A check is drawn on a branch of the depository bank.

Relation to State Law — 12 CFR 229.20

General Rule

Regarding expedited funds availability, 12 CFR 229.20(a) declares how to determine whether Regulation CC or state law takes precedence.

If a state has a shorter hold for a certain category of checks than is provided for under federal law, that state requirement will supersede the federal provision if the state law was effective on or before September 1, 1989. For example, most state laws base some hold periods on whether the check deposited is drawn on an in-state or out-of-state bank. If a state contains more than one check-processing region, the state's hold period for in-state checks may be shorter than the federal maximum hold period for nonlocal checks. Accordingly, the state schedule would supersede the federal schedule to the extent that it applies to in-state, nonlocal checks.

The EFA Act also indicates that any state law providing availability in a shorter period of time than required by federal law applies to all federally insured institutions in that state, including federally chartered institutions. If a state law provides shorter availability only for deposits in accounts in certain categories of banks, such as commercial banks, the superseding state law continues to apply only to those categories of banks, rather than to all federally insured banks in the state.

Civil Liability — 12 CFR 229.21

Statutory Penalties

Individual and class actions can be brought against banks accused of violating part 229's subpart B, Availability of Funds and Disclosure of Funds Availability Policies. 12 CFR 229.21(a) sets forth the statutory penalties that can be imposed when such suits are successful. Basically, a bank could be held liable for:

- Actual damages;
- Not less than $100 nor more than $1,000 in the case of an individual action;

- The lesser of $500,000 or 1 percent of the bank's net worth in a class action; and/or

- The costs of the action together with reasonable attorney's fees as determined by the court.

These penalties also apply to provisions of state law that supersede provisions of this regulation, such as requirements that funds deposited in accounts at banks be made available more promptly than required by this regulation. They do not apply to other provisions of state law. (See commentary to appendix E, 12 CFR 229.20.)

Subpart D — Substitute Checks

General Provisions Governing Substitute Checks — 12 CFR 229.51

A substitute check for which a bank has provided the warranties described in 12 CFR 229.52[1] is the legal equivalent of an original check if the substitute check:

- Accurately represents all of the information on the front and back of the original check; and

- Bears the legend "This is a legal copy of your check. You can use it the same way you would use the original check."[2]

The reconverting bank must adhere to Regulation CC standards for preserving bank endorsements and identifications. A reconverting bank that receives consideration for a substitute check that it transfers, presents, or returns also is the first bank to provide the warranties described in 12 CFR 229.52 and the indemnity described in 12 CFR 229.53.

---

[1] A person other than a bank that creates a substitute check could transfer that check only by agreement unless and until a bank provides the substitute check warranties.

[2] A bank may not vary the language of the legal equivalence legend.

Substitute Check Warranties and Indemnity — 12 CFR 229.52 and 229.53

Starting with the reconverting bank, any bank that transfers, presents, or returns a substitute check (or a paper or electronic representation of a substitute check) and receives consideration for that check warrants that the substitute check meets the legal equivalence requirements and that a check that has already been paid will not be presented for subsequent payment.

Such a bank also provides an indemnity to cover losses that the recipient and any subsequent recipient of the substitute check incurs due to the receipt of a substitute check instead of the original check.

Expedited Recredit for Consumers — 12 CFR 229.54

12 CFR 229.54(a) sets forth the conditions under which a consumer may make an expedited recredit claim for losses associated with the consumer's receipt of a substitute check. To use the expedited recredit procedure, the consumer must be able to assert in good faith that:

- The consumer's account was charged for a substitute check that was provided to the consumer;

- The consumer's account was improperly charged or the consumer has a warranty claim;

- The consumer suffered a loss; and

- The consumer needs the original check or a sufficient copy to determine the validity of the claim.

To make a claim, the consumer must comply with the timing, content, and form requirements in 12 CFR 229.54(b). This section generally provides that the bank holding the consumer's account must receive the consumer's claim by the 40th calendar day following the day the bank mailed the periodic statement describing the contested transaction or the day it mailed the substitute check, whichever is later. The rule applies alternatively to the later of these items' delivery dates, provided the consumer agreed to have the items delivered.

12 CFR 229.54(b)(1)(ii) requires the bank to give the consumer an additional, reasonable period of time if the consumer experiences "extenuating circumstances" that prevent timely submission of the claim. Extenuating circumstances could include the consumer's extended travel or illness.

The commentary to 12 CFR 229.60 provides that the bank may voluntarily give the consumer more time to submit a claim than the rule allows.

Under 12 CFR 229.54(b)(2)(ii), a complaint is not considered complete and thus does not constitute a claim until it contains all of the information the rule requires. The rule requires the claim to contain:[3]

- A description of why the consumer believes the account was improperly charged or the nature of the consumer's warranty claim;

- A statement that the consumer has suffered a loss and an estimate of the amount of the loss;

- A reason why the original check (or a copy of the check that is better than the substitute check the consumer already received) is necessary to determine whether the consumer's claim is valid; and

- Sufficient information to allow the bank to identify the substitute check and investigate the claim.

A bank, in its discretion, may require the consumer to submit the claim in writing. If a consumer makes an oral claim to a bank that requires a written claim, the bank must inform the consumer of the in-writing requirement at that time. Under those circumstances, the bank must receive the written claim by the later of 10 business days from the date of an oral claim or the expiration of the consumer's initial 40-day period for submitting a timely claim. As long as the original oral claim fell within the 40-day requirement for notification and a complete written claim was received within the additional 10-day window, the claim meets the timing requirements (12 CFR 229.54(b)(1) and 229.54(b)(3)), even if the written claim was received after the expiration of the initial 40-day period.

---

[3] If a consumer submits an incomplete complaint, the bank must so inform the consumer and must tell the consumer what information is missing.

The Bank's Action on Claims

12 CFR 229.54(c) requires a bank to act on the consumer's claim no later than the 10th business day after the banking day on which it received the consumer's claim:

- If the bank determines that the consumer's claim is valid, it must recredit the consumer's account no later than the end of the business day following the banking day on which it makes that determination. The recredit should be for the amount of the consumer's loss, up to the amount of the substitute check, plus interest on that amount if the account is an interest-bearing account. The bank must then notify the consumer of the recredit using the notice described in this booklet's "Notices Relating to Expedited Recredit Claims."

- If the bank determines that the consumer's claim is invalid, it must notify the consumer of that decision using the notice described in this booklet's "Notices Relating to Expedited Recredit Claims."

- If the bank has not determined the validity of the consumer's claim by the 10th business day following the banking day on which the bank received the claim, the bank must recredit the consumer's account for the amount of the consumer's loss, up to the amount of the substitute check or $2,500, whichever is less. The bank also must recredit interest on that amount if the consumer's account is an interest-bearing account. The bank must send a notice to that effect to the consumer using the notice described in this booklet's "Notices Relating to Expedited Recredit Claims." If the consumer's loss was more than $2,500, the bank has until the end of the 45th calendar day from the date of the claim to recredit any remaining amount of the consumer's loss, up to the amount of the substitute check (plus interest), unless it determines prior to that time that the claim was invalid and promptly notifies the consumer of that decision.

12 CFR 229.54(d) generally requires that recredited funds receive next day availability. However, a bank that provisionally recredits funds pending further investigation may invoke safeguard exceptions to delay availability of the recredit under the limited circumstances described in 12 CFR 229.54(d)(2). The safeguard exceptions apply to new accounts and repeatedly overdrawn accounts, or when the bank has reasonable cause to suspect the

claim is fraudulent. A bank may delay availability of a provisionally recredited amount until the earlier of the following: 1) the start of the business day after the banking day on which the bank determines the consumer's claim is valid or 2) the 45th calendar day after the banking day on which the bank received the claim if the account is new or overdrawn. If the bank has reasonable cause to believe that the claim is fraudulent, it may delay availability until the 45th calendar day after the banking day on which it received the claim. When the bank delays availability under this section, it may not impose overdraft fees on checks drawn against the provisionally credited funds until the fifth calendar day following the day on which the bank sent the notice regarding the delayed availability.

If, after providing the recredit, the bank determines that the consumer's claim was invalid, the bank may reverse the recredit. This reversal must be accompanied by a consumer notification using the notice discussed below (*Notices Relating to Expedited Recredit Claims*).

Notices Relating to Expedited Recredit Claims

12 CFR 229.54(e) outlines the requirements for providing consumer notices related to expedited recredit:

- The bank must send the notice of recredit no later than the business day after the banking day on which the bank recredits the consumer's account. This notice must include the amount of the recredit and the date the recredited funds will be available for withdrawal.

- The bank must send notice that the consumer's claim is not valid no later than the business day after the banking day on which the bank makes this determination. This notice must include the original check or a sufficient copy of it. (Except as provided in 12 CFR 229.58, see below.) The notice must demonstrate to the consumer why the claim is not valid. The notice also must include either the information or the document that the bank used to make its determination or must state that the consumer may request copies of this information.

- The bank must send the notice of a reversal of recredit no later than the business day following the banking day on which the bank made the reversal. The notice must include all of the information required in a notice of invalid claim plus the amount (including interest) and date of the reversal. 12 CFR 229.54(e)(3).

Appendix C to Regulation CC contains model forms (models C-22 through C-25) that a bank may use to craft the various notices required by 12 CFR 229.54(e). Although no statutory safe harbor for appropriate use of these models exists, the Board published them to assist banks in complying with 12 CFR 229.54(e).

Expedited Recredit for Banks — 12 CFR 229.55

12 CFR 229.55 sets forth expedited recredit procedures between banks. A claimant bank must adhere to the timing, content, and form requirements of 12 CFR 229.55(b) in order for the claim to be valid. A bank against which an interbank recredit claim is made has 10 business days to act on the claim (12 CFR 229.55(c)). The provisions of 12 CFR 229.55 may vary by agreement. (No other provisions of subpart D may vary by agreement.)

Liability — 12 CFR 229.56

12 CFR 229.56 describes the damages for which a bank or person would be liable in the event of breach of warranty or failure to comply with subpart D:

- The amount of the actual loss, up to the amount of the substitute check, resulting from the breach or failure, and

- Interest and expenses (including costs, reasonable attorney's fees, and other expenses of representation) related to the substitute check.

These amounts could be reduced in the event of negligence or failure to act in good faith. It is also important to note that 12 CFR 229.56 has a specific exception that allows for greater recovery as provided in the indemnity section. Thus, a person that had an indemnity claim that also involves a breach of a substitute check warranty could recover all damages proximately caused by the warranty breach.

12 CFR 229.56(b) excuses failure to meet this subpart's time limits because of circumstances beyond a bank's control. 12 CFR 229.56(c) provides that an

action to enforce a claim under this subpart may be brought in any United States district court.

12 CFR 229.56(c) also provides the subpart's statute of limitations: one year from the date on which a person's cause of action accrues.[4] 12 CFR 229.56(d) states that if a person fails to provide notice of a claim for more than 30 days from the date on which a cause of action accrues, the warranting or indemnifying bank is discharged from liability *to the extent of any loss caused by the delay in giving notice of the claim.*

Consumer Awareness —12 CFR 229.57

Contents of Disclosures

A bank must provide its consumer customers with a disclosure that explains that a substitute check is the legal equivalent of the original check and describes the consumer's recredit rights for substitute checks. A bank may, but is not required to, use the Board's model form (model C-5A in appendix C to Regulation CC) to meet the content requirements for this notice. A bank that uses the model form appropriately is deemed to be in compliance with the content requirements for which it uses language from the model form. In its disclosure, a bank may provide additional information relating to substitute checks.

Distribution of Disclosures

Distribution to consumer customers who receive canceled checks with periodic account statements. Under 12 CFR 229.57(b)(1), a bank must provide the disclosure upon establishing a relationship with a new consumer customer who will routinely receive canceled checks in periodic statements.

Distribution to consumer customers who occasionally receive a substitute check. Under 12 CFR 229.57(b)(2), a bank must provide the disclosure to a consumer customer who occasionally receives a substitute check. Consumers who receive disclosures include those who receive a substitute check in

---

[4] For purposes of this paragraph, a cause of action accrues as of the date on which the injured person first learns, or reasonably should have learned, of the facts giving rise to the claim, including the identity of the warranting or indemnifying bank against which the action is brought.

response to a request for a check or a copy of a check, and those who receive a substitute check in place of an unpaid check they have deposited. If the bank previously provided the disclosure to these consumers, it must do so again.

When the consumer contacts the bank to request a check or a copy of a check and the bank responds by providing a substitute check, the bank must provide this disclosure at the time of the request, if feasible. Otherwise, the bank must provide the disclosure no later than when the bank provides a substitute check in response to the consumer's request. It would not be feasible to provide the disclosure at the time of the request if, for example, the consumer made his or her request by telephone or if the bank did not know at the time of the request whether it would provide a substitute check or some other document in response. A bank is not required to provide the disclosure if the bank responds to the consumer's request by providing something other than an actual substitute check (such as a photocopy of an original check or a substitute check).

When a bank returns a deposited item unpaid to a consumer in the form of a substitute check, the bank must provide the disclosure when it provides the substitute check.

Mode of Delivery of Information — 12 CFR 229.58

12 CFR 229.58 provides that banks may deliver any notice or other information required under this subpart by United States mail or by any other means to which the recipient has agreed to receive account information, including electronically. A bank that is required to provide an original check or a sufficient copy (each of which is defined as a specific paper document) may provide an electronic image of the original check or sufficient copy instead, if the recipient has agreed to receive that information electronically.

Laws
12 USC 4001, Expedited Funds Availability Act

Regulations
12 CFR 229, Expedited Funds Availability Regulation

OCC Issuances
OCC Bulletin 2004-49, "Check Clearing for the 21st Century Act (Check 21) and 12 CFR 229, Availability of Funds and Collection of Checks (Regulations CC): Availability of FFIEC's InfoBase for Check 21 and Updated Examination Procedures for Regulation CC"

Truth in Savings

Background and Summary

Regulation DD (12 CFR 230), which implements the Truth in Savings Act (TISA), became effective in June 1993. An official staff commentary interprets the requirements of Regulation DD (12 CFR 230 (Supplement I)). Since then, several amendments have been made to Regulation DD and the Staff Commentary, including changes, effective January 1, 2010, concerning disclosures of aggregate overdraft and returned item fees on periodic statements and balance disclosures provided to consumers through automated systems. In addition, effective July 6, 2010, clarifications were made to the provisions related to overdraft services (**NOTE:** The effective date for the clarification to section 230.11(a)(1)(i), requiring the term "Total Overdraft Fees" to be used, is October 1, 2010) (75 FR 31673).

The purpose of Regulation DD is to enable consumers to make informed decisions about their accounts at depository institutions through the use of uniform disclosures. The disclosures aid comparison shopping by informing consumers about the fees, annual percentage yield, interest rate, and other terms for deposit accounts. A consumer is entitled to receive disclosures:

- When an account is opened;
- Upon request;
- When the terms of the account are changed;
- When a periodic statement is sent; and
- For most time accounts, before the account matures.

The regulation also includes requirements on the payment of interest, the methods of calculating the balance on which interest is paid, the calculation of the annual percentage yield, and advertising.

Coverage (12 CFR 230.1)

Regulation DD applies to all depository institutions, except credit unions, that offer deposit accounts to residents of any state. Branches of foreign institutions located in the United States are subject to Regulation DD if they offer deposit accounts to consumers. Edge Act and agreement corporations, and agencies of foreign institutions, are not depository institutions for purposes of Regulation DD.

In addition, persons who advertise accounts are subject to the advertising rules. For example, if a deposit broker places an advertisement offering consumers an interest in an account at a depository institution, the advertising rules apply to the advertisement, whether the account is to be held by the broker or directly by the consumer.

Definitions (12 CFR 230.2)

Section 230.2 defines key terms used in Regulation DD. Among those definitions are the following:

Account (section 230.2(a)) — a deposit account at a depository institution that is held by or offered to a consumer. It includes time, demand, savings, and negotiable order of withdrawal accounts. Regulation DD covers interest-bearing as well as noninterest-bearing accounts.

Advertisement (section 230.2(b)) — a commercial message, appearing in any medium, that promotes directly or indirectly (a) the availability or terms of, or a deposit in, a new account, and (b) for purposes of sections 230.8(a) (misleading or inaccurate advertisements) and 230.11 (additional disclosure requirements for institutions advertising the payment of overdrafts), the terms of, or a deposit in, a new or existing account. An advertisement includes a commercial message in visual, oral, or print media that invites, offers, or otherwise announces generally to prospective customers the availability or terms of, or a deposit in, a consumer account. Examples of advertisements include telephone solicitations and messages on automated teller machine screens.

Annual percentage yield (section 230.2(c)) — a percentage rate reflecting the total amount of interest paid on an account, based on the interest rate and the frequency of compounding for a 365-day period or 366-day period during leap years and calculated according to the rules in appendix A of Regulation DD. Interest or other earnings are not to be included in the annual percentage yield if the circumstances for determining the interest and other earnings may or may not occur in the future (see appendix A, footnote 1).

Average daily balance method (section 230.2(d)) — the application of a periodic rate to the average daily balance in the account for the period. The average daily balance is determined by adding the full amount of principal in the account for each day of the period and dividing that figure by the number of days in the period.

Board (section 230.2(e)) — the Board of Governors of the Federal Reserve System.

Bonus (section 230.2(f)) — a premium, gift, award, or other consideration worth more than $10 (whether in the form of cash, credit, merchandise, or any equivalent) given or offered to a consumer during a year in exchange for opening, maintaining, renewing, or increasing an account balance. The term does not include interest, other consideration worth $10 or less given during a year, the waiver or reduction of a fee, or the absorption of expenses.

Business day (section 230.2(g)) — a calendar day other than a Saturday, a Sunday, or any of the legal public holidays specified in 5 USC 6103(a).

Consumer (section 230.2(h)) — a natural person who holds an account primarily for personal, family, or household purposes, or to whom such an account is offered. The term does not include accounts held by a natural person on behalf of another in a professional capacity or accounts held by individuals as sole proprietors.

Daily balance method (section 230.2(i)) — the application of a daily periodic rate to the full amount of principal in the account each day.

Depository institution and institution (section 230.2(j)) — an institution as defined in section 19(b)(1)(A)(i)-(vi) of the Federal Reserve Act (12 USC 461), except credit unions defined in section 19(b)(1)(A)(iv). Branches of foreign institutions located in the United States are subject to the regulation if they offer deposit accounts to consumers. Edge Act and agreement corporations, and agencies of foreign institutions, are not depository institutions for purposes of this regulation.

Deposit broker (section 230.2(k)) — a person who is in the business of placing or facilitating the placement of deposits in an institution, as defined by section 29(g) of the Federal Deposit Insurance Act (12 USC 1831f(g)).

Fixed-rate account (section 230.2(l)) — an account for which the institution contracts to give at least 30 calendar days' advance written notice of decreases in the interest rate.

Grace period (section 230.2(m)) — a period following the maturity of an automatically renewing time account during which the consumer may withdraw funds without being assessed a penalty.

Interest (section 230.2(n)) — any payment to a consumer or to an account for the use of funds in an account, calculated by applying a periodic rate to the balance. Interest does not include the payment of a bonus or other consideration worth $10 or less during a year, the waiver or reduction of a fee, or the absorption of expenses.

Interest rate (section 230.2(o)) — the annual rate of interest paid on an account and does not reflect compounding. For purposes of the account disclosures in section 230.4(b)(1)(i), the interest rate may, but need not, be referred to as the "annual percentage rate" in addition to being referred to as the "interest rate."

Passbook savings account (section 230.2(p)) — a savings account in which the consumer retains a book or other document in which the institution records transactions on the account. Passbook savings accounts include accounts accessed by preauthorized electronic fund transfers to the account. As defined in Regulation E, a preauthorized electronic fund transfer is an electronic fund transfer authorized in advance to recur at substantially regular intervals. Examples include an account that receives direct deposit of Social Security payments. Accounts permitting access by other electronic means are not passbook savings accounts and must comply with the requirements of section 230.6 if statements are sent four or more times a year.

Periodic statement (section 230.2(q)) — a statement setting forth information about an account (other than a time account or passbook savings account) that is provided to a consumer on a regular basis four or more times a year.

State (section 230.2(r)) — a state of the United States, the District of Columbia, the commonwealth of Puerto Rico, and any territory or possession of the United States.

Stepped-rate account (section 230.2(s)) — an account that has two or more interest rates that take effect in succeeding periods and are known when the account is opened.

Tiered-rate account (section 230.2(t)) — an account that has two or more interest rates that are applicable to specified balance levels. A requirement to maintain a minimum balance to earn interest does not make an account a tiered-rate account.

Time account (section 230.2(u)) — an account with a maturity of at least seven days in which the consumer generally does not have a right to make withdrawals for six days after the account is opened, unless the deposit is subject to an early withdrawal penalty of at least seven days' interest on the amount withdrawn.

Variable-rate account (section 230.2(v)) — an account whose interest rate may change after the account is opened, unless the institution contracts to give at least 30 calendar days' advance written notice of rate decreases.

General Disclosure Requirements (12 CFR 230.3)

General Requirements (Section 230.3(a) and (b))

Section 230.3 outlines the general requirements for account disclosures and periodic-statement disclosures. Such disclosures are required to be:

- Clear and conspicuous.
- In writing.
- In a form the consumer may keep.

- Clearly identifiable for different accounts, if disclosures for different accounts are combined.

- Reflective of the terms of the legal obligation in the account agreement between the consumer and the depository institution.

- Available in English upon request if the disclosures are made in languages other than English.

- Consistent in terminology when describing terms or features that are required to be disclosed.

Electronic Disclosures

Regulation DD disclosures may be provided to the consumer in electronic form, subject to compliance with the consumer consent and other applicable provisions of the Electronic Signatures in Global and National Commerce Act (E-Sign Act) (15 USC 7001 et seq.).

The E-Sign Act does not mandate that institutions or consumers use or accept electronic records or signatures. It does, however, permit institutions to satisfy any statutory or regulatory requirements that information, such as Regulation DD disclosures, be provided in writing to a consumer by providing the information electronically after obtaining the consumer's affirmative consent. But before consent can be given, consumers must be provided with a clear and conspicuous statement informing the consumer of:

- Any right or option to have the information provided in paper or nonelectronic form;

- The right to withdraw the consent to receive information electronically and the consequences, including fees, of doing so;

- The scope of the consent (whether the consent applies only to a particular transaction or to identified categories of records that may be provided during the course of the parties' relationship);

- The procedures to withdraw consent and to update information needed to contact the consumer electronically; and

- The methods by which a consumer may obtain, upon request, a paper copy of an electronic record after consent has been given to receive the information electronically and whether any fee will be charged.

Prior to consenting, the consumer must be provided with a statement of the hardware and software requirements for access to and retention of the electronic information. The consumer must consent electronically or confirm consent electronically in a manner that "reasonably demonstrates that the consumer can access information in the electronic form that will be used to provide the information that is the subject of the consent."

After the consent, if an institution changes the hardware or software requirements such that a consumer may be prevented from accessing and retaining information electronically, the institution must notify the consumer of the new requirements and must allow the consumer to withdraw consent without charge.

Under section 230.3(a), the disclosures required by sections 230.4(a)(2) (Disclosures Upon Request) and 230.8 (Advertising) may be provided to the consumer in electronic form without regard to the consumer consent or other provisions of the E-Sign Act, as set forth in those sections of Regulation DD. For example, under section 230.4(a)(2) (Disclosures Upon Request), if a consumer who is not present at the institution makes a request for disclosures, the institution may provide the disclosures electronically if the consumer agrees without regard to the consumer consent or other provisions of the E-Sign Act.

Relation to Regulation E (Section 230.3(c))

Disclosures required by and provided in accordance with the Electronic Fund Transfer Act (15 USC 1693 *et seq.*) and its implementing Regulation E (12 CFR 205) that are also required by Regulation DD may be substituted for the disclosures required by this regulation. Compliance with Regulation E (12 CFR 205) is deemed to satisfy the disclosure requirements of Regulation DD, such as when

- An institution changes a term that triggers a notice under Regulation E, and uses the timing and disclosure rules of Regulation E for sending change-in-term notices.

- Consumers add an ATM access feature to an account, and the institution provides disclosures pursuant to Regulation E, including disclosure of fees (see 12 CFR 205.7).

- An institution, complying with the timing rules of Regulation E, discloses at the same time fees for electronic services (such as for balance inquiry fees at ATMs) required to be disclosed by this regulation but not by Regulation E.

- An institution relies on Regulation E's rules regarding disclosure of limits on the frequency and amount of electronic fund transfers, including security-related exceptions. But any limits on intra-institutional transfers to or from the consumer's other accounts during a given time period must be disclosed, even though intra-institutional transfers are exempt from Regulation E.

Other Requirements (Section 230.3(d) – (f))

Other general disclosure requirements include the following:

Multiple Consumers (section 230.3(d))

If an account is held by more than one consumer, disclosures may be made to any one of the consumers.

Oral Response to a Rate Inquiry (section 230.3(e))

If an institution chooses to provide rate information orally, it must state the annual percentage yield and may state the interest rate. However, the institution may not state any other rate. The advertising rules do not cover an oral response to a rate inquiry.

Rounding and Accuracy Rules for Rates and Yields (section 230.3(f))

The rounding and accuracy requirements are as follows:

- Rounding — The annual percentage yield, the annual percentage yield earned, and the interest rate must be rounded to the nearest one-hundredth of one percentage point (0.01 percent) and expressed to two decimal places. (For account disclosures, the interest rate may be expressed to more than two decimal places.) For example, if an annual percentage yield is calculated at 5.644 percent, it must be rounded down and disclosed as 5.64 percent, or if annual percentage yield is calculated at 5.645 percent, it must be rounded up and disclosed as 5.65 percent.

- Accuracy — The annual percentage yield (and the annual percentage yield earned) will be considered accurate if it is not more that one-twentieth of one percentage point (0.05 percent) above or below the annual percentage yield (and the annual percentage yield earned) that are calculated in accordance with appendix A of Regulation DD.

Account Disclosures (12 CFR 230.4)

Section 230.4 covers the delivery and content of account disclosures both at the time an account is opened and when requested by a consumer.

Delivery of Account Disclosures (Section 230.4(a))

Disclosures at Account Opening. 230.4(a)(1)

A depository institution must provide account disclosures to a consumer before an account is opened or a service is provided, whichever is earlier. (An institution is deemed to have provided a service when a fee, required to be disclosed, is assessed.)

If the consumer is not present when the account is opened or the service is provided and has not received disclosures; an institution must mail or deliver the account opening disclosures no later than 10 business days after the account is opened or the service is provided, whichever is earlier.

If a consumer who is not present at the institution uses electronic means (for example, an Internet Web site) to apply to open an account or to request a service, the disclosures must be provided before the account is opened or the service is provided.

Disclosures upon Request. 230.4(a)(2)

A depository institution must provide full account disclosures, including complete fee schedules, to a consumer upon request. Institutions must comply with all requests for this information, whether or not the requestor is an existing customer or a prospective customer. A response to an oral inquiry (by telephone or in person) about rates and yields or fees does not trigger the duty to provide account disclosures. However, when consumers ask for written information about an account (whether by telephone, in person, or by other means), the institution must provide disclosures, unless the account is no longer offered to the public.

If the consumer makes the request in person, disclosures must be provided at that time. If a consumer is not present when the request is made, the institution must mail or deliver the disclosures within a reasonable time after it receives the request. Ten business days is considered a reasonable time for responding to requests for account information that a consumer does not make in person, including requests made by electronic means (such as by electronic mail).

If a consumer who is not present at the institution makes a request for account disclosures, including a request made by telephone, by e-mail, or via the institution's Web site, the institution may send the disclosures in paper form or, if the consumer agrees, may provide the disclosures electronically, such as to an e-mail address that the consumer provides for that purpose, or on the institution's Web site, without regard to the consumer consent or other provisions of the E-Sign Act. The institution is not required to provide the disclosures required by section 230.4(a)(2) in electronic form, nor is the consumer required to agree to receive them in that form.

When providing disclosures upon the request of a consumer, the institution may choose any of several ways of rendering the interest rate and annual percentage yield. It may do so:

- As of the most recent seven calendar days,

- As of an identified date, or

- As of the current date, by providing a telephone number for consumers to call.

Further, when providing disclosures upon the request of a consumer, the institution may state the maturity of a time account as a term rather than a date. Describing the maturity of a time account as "one year" or "six months," for example, illustrates a statement of the maturity as a term rather than a date ("January 10, 1995").

Content of Account Disclosures (Section 230.4(b))

Account disclosures must include, as applicable, information on the following (see appendix A and B of Regulation DD for information on the annual percentage yield calculation and for model clauses for account disclosures and sample forms):

te ⬜⬜⬜ *t*⬜⬜ ⬜*se*⬜ *t*⬜ ⬜⬜⬜.⬜⬜ ⬜⬜⬜
An institution must disclose both the "annual percentage yield" and the "interest rate," using those terms.

For fixed-rate accounts, an institution must disclose the period of time that the interest rate will be in effect.

For variable-rate accounts, an institution must disclose the following:

• The fact that the interest rate and annual percentage yield may change,

• How the interest rate is determined,

• The frequency with which the interest rate may change, and

• Any limitation on the amount the interest rate may change.

⬜⬜⬜ ⬜⬜⬜⬜⬜⬜ ⬜⬜⬜ ⬜⬜*e*⬜ *t*⬜ ⬜*se*⬜ *t*⬜ ⬜⬜⬜.⬜⬜ ⬜⬜⬜
An institution must disclose the frequency with which interest is compounded and credited. If consumers will forfeit interest if they close an account before accrued interest is credited, an institution must state that interest will not be paid.

⬜⬜⬜⬜*e* ⬜⬜⬜ ⬜*t*⬜ ⬜*se*⬜ *t*⬜ ⬜⬜⬜.⬜⬜ ⬜⬜⬜
An institution must disclose the following information about account balances:

• Minimum balance requirements required to:
  – Open the account,

  – Avoid the imposition of a fee, or

  – Obtain the annual percentage yield disclosed.

  In addition, the institution must disclose how the balance is determined to avoid the imposition of a fee or to obtain the annual percentage yield.

- An explanation of the balance-computation method, specified in section 230.7 of Regulation DD, that is used to calculate interest on the account. An institution may use different methods or periods to calculate minimum balances for purposes of imposing a fee and accruing interest. Each method and corresponding period must be disclosed.

- When interest begins to accrue on noncash deposits.

Fees (section 230.4(b)(4))

An institution must disclose the amount of any fee that may be imposed in connection with the account (or an explanation of how the fee will be determined) and the conditions under which the fee may be imposed. Examples of fees that must be disclosed are:

- Maintenance fees, such as monthly service fees,

- Fees to open or to close an account,

- Fees related to deposits or withdrawals, such as fees for use of the institution's ATMs, and

- Fees for special services, such as stop-payment fees.

Institutions must state if fees that may be assessed against an account are tied to other accounts at the institution. For example, if an institution ties the fees payable on a NOW account to balances held in the NOW account and a savings account, the NOW account disclosures must state that fact and explain how the fee is determined.

An institution must specify the categories of transactions for which an overdraft fee may be imposed. For example, it is sufficient to state that the fee applies to overdrafts "created by check, in-person withdrawal, ATM withdrawal, or other electronic means." However, it is insufficient to state that a fee applies "for overdraft items."

Transaction limitations (section 230.4(b)(5))

An institution must disclose any limitations on the number or dollar amount of withdrawals or deposits. Examples of such limitations include:

- Limits on the number of checks that may be written on an account within a given time period,

- Limits on withdrawals or deposits during the term of a time account, and

- Limits under Regulation D (Reserve Requirements on Depository Institutions) on the number of withdrawals permitted from money market deposit accounts by check to third parties each month.

 e t es   t e   ts se t   .

For time accounts, an institution must disclose information about the following features:

- Time requirements — An institution must state the maturity date and, for "callable" time accounts, the date or circumstances under which an institution may redeem a time account at the institution's option.

- Early withdrawal penalties — An institution must state:

  - Whether a penalty will or may be imposed for early withdrawal,

  - How it is calculated, and

  - The conditions for its assessment.

  - An institution may, but does not need to, use the term "penalty" to describe the loss of interest that consumers may incur for early withdrawal of funds from an account.

  Examples of early withdrawal penalties include:

  - Monetary penalties, such as "$10.00" or "seven days' interest plus accrued but uncredited interest,"

  - Adverse changes to terms such as a lowering of the interest rate, annual percentage yield, or compounding frequency for funds remaining on deposit, and

  - Reclamation of bonuses.

- Withdrawal of interest prior to maturity — an institution must disclose the following, as applicable:

- That the annual percentage yield assumes interest remains on deposit until maturity and that a withdrawal will reduce earnings for accounts whose:

    ▪ Compounding occurs during the term, and

    ▪ Interest may be withdrawn prior to maturity.

- That interest cannot remain on deposit and that payout of interest is mandatory for accounts whose:

    ▪ Stated maturity is greater than one year,

    ▪ Interest is not compounded on an annual or more frequent basis,

    ▪ Interest is required to be paid out at least annually, and

    ▪ Annual percentage yield is determined in accordance with section E of appendix A of Regulation DD.

- Renewal policies — An institution must state whether an account will, or will not, renew automatically at maturity. If it will, the statement must indicate whether a grace period will be provided and, if so, must indicate the length of that period. For accounts that do not renew automatically, the statement must indicate whether interest will be paid after maturity if the consumer does not renew the account.

*ses se t . *
For bonuses, an institution must disclose:

- The amount or type of any bonus,

- When the bonus will be provided, and

- Any minimum balance and time requirements to obtain the bonus.

Subsequent Disclosures (12 CFR 230.5)

Section 230.5 covers the required disclosures when the terms of an account change, resulting in a negative effect on the consumer. In addition, this section covers the required disclosures for both time accounts that automatically renew and have a maturity longer than one month and time accounts that do not renew automatically and have a maturity of longer than one year.

Change in Terms (Section 230.5(a))

e t e eq e se t .
An institution must give advance notice to affected consumers of any change in a term that is required to be disclosed if the change may reduce the annual percentage yield or adversely affect the consumer. The notice must include the effective date of the change and must be mailed or delivered at least 30 calendar days before the effective date of the change.

 t e eq e se t .
An institution is not required to provide a notice for the following changes:

- For variable-rate accounts, any change in the interest rate and corresponding changes in the annual percentage yield,

- Any changes in fees assessed for check printing,

- For short-term time accounts, any changes in any term for accounts with maturities of one month or less,

- The imposition of account maintenance or activity fees that previously had been waived for a consumer when the consumer was employed by the depository institution, but who is no longer employed there, and

- The expiration of a one-year period that was part of a promotion, described in the account-opening disclosures — for example, to "waive $4.00 monthly service charges for one year."

Notice for Time Accounts Longer Than One Month That Renew Automatically (Section 230.5(b))

For automatically renewing time accounts with maturity longer than one month, an institution must provide different disclosures depending on whether the maturity is longer than one year or one year or less. All disclosures must be provided e e maturity. The requirements are summarized below and in a chart at the end of this section.

If the maturity is longer than one year, the institution must provide the date the existing account matures and the required account disclosures for a new account, as described in section 230.4(b). If the interest rate and annual percentage yield that will be paid for the new account are unknown when disclosures are provided, the institution must state:

- That those rates have not yet been determined,

- The date when they will be determined, and

- A telephone number for consumers to call to obtain the interest rate and the annual percentage yield for the new account.

If the maturity is longer than one month but less than or equal to one year, the institution must either:

- Provide the disclosures required in section 230.5(b)(1) for accounts longer than one year, or

- Disclose to the consumer:

  - The date the existing account matures and the new maturity date if the account is renewed.

  - The interest rate and the annual percentage yield for the new account if they are known. If the rates have not yet been determined, the institution must disclose:

    - The date when they will be determined, and

    - A telephone number the consumer may call to obtain the interest rate and the annual percentage yield for the new account.

  - Any difference between the terms of the new account and the terms required to be disclosed for the existing account.

§ 230.5(b)(1)(ii)

All disclosures must be mailed or delivered at least 30 calendar days before maturity of the existing account. Alternatively, the disclosures may be mailed or delivered at least 20 calendar days before the end of the grace period on the existing account, provided a grace period of at least five calendar days is allowed.

§ 230.5(b)(2) [Maturities longer than one year that do not renew automatically (Section 230.5(b)(2))]

For time accounts with maturity longer than one year that do not renew automatically at maturity, an institution must disclose to consumers the maturity date and whether interest will be paid after maturity. The disclosures must be mailed or delivered at least 10 calendar days before maturity of the existing account. The requirements are summarized in a chart in attachment A of these procedures.

Periodic Statement Disclosures (12 CFR 230.6)

Regulation DD does not require institutions to provide periodic statements. However, for institutions that mail or deliver periodic statements, section 230.6 sets forth specific information that must be included in a periodic statement.

General Requirements (Section 230.6(a))

The statement must include the following disclosures:

§ 230.6(a)(1) [Annual percentage yield earned (Section 230.6(a)(1))]

An institution must state the annual percentage yield earned during the statement period, using that term, and calculated according to Appendix A of Regulation DD.

§ 230.6(a)(2) [Amount of interest (Section 230.6(a)(2))]

An institution must state the dollar amount of interest earned during the statement period, whether or not it was credited. In disclosing interest earned for the period, an institution must use the term "interest" or terminology such as:

- "Interest paid" to describe interest that has been credited, or

- "Interest accrued" or "interest earned" to indicate that interest is not yet credited.

Fees [illegible] se [illegible]se [illegible] [illegible].[illegible]

An institution must report any fees that are required to be disclosed and that were debited to the account during the statement period, even if assessed for an earlier period. The fees must be itemized by type and dollar amounts. When fees of the same type are imposed more than once in a statement period, an institution may itemize each fee separately or group the fees together and disclose a total dollar amount for all fees of that type. When fees of the same type are grouped together, the description must make clear that the dollar figure represents more than a single fee, for example, "total fees for checks written this period." The Staff Commentary provides examples of fees that may not be grouped together. For example, an institution must separately identify whether a fee was for the payment of an overdraft or for returning the item unpaid.

Total overdraft and returned item fees, if any, must also be disclosed on the periodic statement. An institution must provide totals for fees for the payment of overdrafts and totals for items returned unpaid, both for the statement period and for the calendar year to date. See section 230.11(a)(1) and (2). (The institution may, however, continue to itemize overdraft and returned item fees.)

[illegible]e[illegible] t[illegible] [illegible]e[illegible] [illegible]se[illegible] t[illegible] [illegible].[illegible]

An institution must indicate the total number of days in the statement period, or the beginning and ending dates of the period. Institutions providing the beginning and ending dates of the period must make clear whether both dates are included in the period.

[illegible] [illegible]e[illegible] st[illegible]te[illegible] e[illegible]ts [illegible]st[illegible] [illegible]e[illegible] t[illegible] [illegible]se[illegible] t[illegible] [illegible].[illegible]

Institutions may provide information about an account (for example, a money market deposit account) on the periodic statement for another account (such as a negotiable order of withdrawal account) without triggering the disclosures required by this section, as long as:

- The information is limited to the account number, the type of account, or balance information, and

- The institution also provides a periodic statement complying with this section for each account.

*e te ee s s e . *

If an institution charges a consumer overdraft and returned item fees, it must disclose them on the consumer's periodic statement as required by section 230.11(a).

Special Rule for Average Daily Balance Method (Section 230.6(b))

Section 230.6 has special periodic statement requirements for an institution using the average daily balance method and calculating interest for a period other than the statement period. In these situations, an institution must calculate and disclose the annual percentage yield earned and amount of interest earned based on the time period used rather than the statement period. In addition, when disclosing the length of period requirement on the periodic statement, an institution must state this information for the statement period as well as the interest-calculation period. (See staff commentary for examples.)

Payment of Interest (Section 230.7)

Section 230.7 covers the payment of interest, including how to determine the balance on which to pay interest, the daily periodic rate to use, and the date interest begins to accrue.

Permissible Methods To Determine Balance To Calculate Interest (Section 230.7(a)(1))

An institution must calculate interest on the full amount of principal in an account for each day by using one of the two following methods:

- Daily balance method, which applies the daily periodic rate to the full amount of principal in the account each day, or

- Average daily balance method, which applies a periodic rate to the average daily balance in the account for the period. The average daily balance is determined by adding the full amount of principal in the account for each day of the period and dividing that figure by the number of days in the period.

The following are prohibited calculation methods:

- Ending-balance method, whereby interest is paid on the balance in the account at the end of the period,

- Low-balance method, whereby interest is paid based on the lowest balance in the account for any day in that period, and

- Investable-balance method, whereby interest is paid on a percentage of the balance, excluding the amount set aside for reserve requirements.

Institutions may apply a daily periodic rate greater than 1/365 of the interest rate—such as 1/360 of the interest rate—as long as it is applied 365 days a year.

Institutions may apply a daily rate of 1/366 or 1/365 of the interest rate for 366 days in a leap year, if the account will earn interest for February 29.

Institutions are not required to pay interest after time accounts mature.

Institutions must pay interest on funds in an account, even if inactivity or the infrequency of transactions would permit the institution to consider the account to be "inactive" or "dormant" (or similar status) as defined by state laws, other laws, or the account contract.

Permissible Methods To Determine Minimum Balance To Earn Interest (Section 230.7(a)(2))

If an institution requires a minimum balance to earn interest, it must use the same method to determine the required minimum balance as it uses to determine the balance on which interest is calculated. For example, if an institution requires a $300 minimum balance that would be determined by using the average daily balance method, then it must calculate interest based on the average daily balance method. Further, an institution may use an additional method that is unequivocally beneficial to the consumer.

An institution that requires a minimum balance may choose not to pay interest for days or a period when the balance drops below the required minimum, whether they use the daily balance method or the average daily balance method to calculate interest.

Institutions must pay interest on the full balance in any account that meets the required minimum balance. For example, if $300 is the minimum daily balance required to earn interest, and a consumer deposits $500, the institution must pay the stated interest rate on the full $500 and not just on $200.

Institutions may use the daily balance method, the average daily balance method, or any other computation method to calculate minimum balance requirements that do not involve the payment of interest. For example, an institution may use any computation method to compute minimum balances for assessing fees.

Compounding and Crediting Policies (Section 230.7(b))

This section does not require institutions to compound or credit interest at any particular frequency. Institutions choosing to compound interest may compound or credit interest annually, semi-annually, quarterly, monthly, daily, continuously, or on any other basis.

An institution may choose not to pay accrued interest if consumers close an account prior to the date accrued interest is credited, as long as the institution has disclosed this practice in the initial account disclosures.

Date Interest Begins To Accrue (Section 230.7(c))

Interest shall begin to accrue not later than the business day specified for interest-bearing accounts in section 606 of the Expedited Funds Availability Act, which states that:

> Interest shall accrue on funds deposited in an interest-bearing account at a depository institution beginning not later than the business day on which the depository institution receives provisional credit for such funds.

Interest shall accrue until the day funds are withdrawn.

Advertising (12 CFR 230.8)

Section 230.8 contains account advertising requirements, including overall general rules and rules for special account features. In addition, the section describes advertising involving certain types of media and in-house posters that are exempt from Regulation DD's advertising requirements.

General Advertising Rules (Section 230.8(a) and (b))

An institution may not advertise in a way that is misleading or inaccurate or misrepresents its deposit contract. In addition, an advertisement may not use the word "profit" in referring to interest paid on an account.

An institution's advertisement may not refer to or describe an account as "free" or "no cost" (or contain a similar term such as "fees waived") if a maintenance or activity fee may be imposed on the account. Examples of such maintenance or activity fees include:

- Any fee imposed when a minimum-balance requirement is not met, or when consumers exceed a specified number of transactions;

- Transaction and service fees that consumers reasonably expect to be imposed on a regular basis;

- A flat fee, such as a monthly service fee; and

- Fees imposed to deposit, withdraw, or transfer funds, including per-check or per-transaction charges (for example, 25 cents for each withdrawal, whether by check or in person).

Examples of fees that are not maintenance or activity fees include:

- Fees not required to be disclosed under section 230.4(b)(4),

- Check-printing fees,

- Balance-inquiry fees,

- Stop-payment fees and fees associated with checks returned unpaid,

- Fees assessed against a dormant account, and

- Fees for ATM or electronic transfer services (such as preauthorized transfers or home banking services) not required to obtain an account.

If an account (or a specific account service) is free only for a limited period of time (for example, for one year following the account opening), the account (or service) may be advertised as free if the time period is also stated.

If an electronic advertisement (such as an advertisement appearing on an Internet Web site) displays a triggering term (such as a bonus or annual percentage yield) described elsewhere in section 230.8, the advertisement must clearly refer the consumer to the location where the additional required information begins. For example, an advertisement that includes a bonus or annual percentage yield may be accompanied by a link that directly takes the consumer to the additional information. As discussed in section 230.3(a), electronic advertising disclosures may be provided to the consumer in electronic form without regard to the consumer consent or other provisions of the E-Sign Act.

The staff commentary provides the following examples of advertisements that would ordinarily be misleading, inaccurate, or misrepresent the deposit contract:

- Representing an overdraft service as a "line of credit," unless the service is subject to the Board's Regulation Z, 12 CFR 226.

- Representing that the institution will honor all checks or authorize payment of all transactions that overdraw an account, with or without a specified dollar limit, when the institution retains discretion at any time not to honor checks or authorize transactions.

- Representing that consumers with an overdrawn account are allowed to maintain a negative balance when the terms of the account's overdraft service require consumers promptly to return the deposit account to a positive balance.

- Describing an institution's overdraft service solely as protection against bounced checks when the institution also permits overdrafts for a fee when accounts are overdrawn by other means, such as ATM withdrawals, debit card transactions, or other electronic fund transfers.

- Advertising an account-related service for which the institution charges a fee in an advertisement that also uses the word "free" or "no cost" (or a similar term) to describe the account, unless the advertisement clearly and conspicuously indicates that there is a cost associated with the service. If the fee is a maintenance or activity fee under section 230.8(a)(2) of this part, however, an advertisement may not describe the account as "free" or "no cost" (or contain a similar term) even if the fee is disclosed in the advertisement.

Rate of Return Disclosure

When an institution states a rate of return in an advertisement:

- It must state the rate as an "annual percentage yield," using that term.

- If the advertisement uses the abbreviation "APY," the term "annual percentage yield" must be stated at least once in the advertisement.

- If the advertisement uses the term "interest rate," it must use the term in conjunction with, but not more conspicuously than, the related annual percentage yield.

- It may not state any other rate except "annual percentage yield" or "interest rate."

- It must round the annual percentage yield, the annual percentage yield earned, and the interest rate to the nearest one-hundredth of one percentage point (0.01 percent) and express them to two decimal places.

An advertisement for a tiered-rate account that states an annual percentage yield must also state the annual percentage yield for each tier, along with corresponding minimum-balance requirements.

An advertisement for a stepped-rate account that states an interest rate must state all the interest rates and the time period that each rate is in effect.

Required Advertising for Special Account Features (Section 230.8(c))

If an institution advertises an annual percentage yield for a product and the product includes one of the features listed in sections 230.8(c)(1)-(6), then the institution must clearly and conspicuously disclose the information outlined in sections 230.8(c)(1)-(6), as noted below. However, these requirements do not necessarily apply if the situation falls under the exemptions of section 230.8(e).

□□□□□□e □□ tes □se□ t□ □ □□□.□□□□□
For variable-rate accounts, the advertisement must state that the rate may change after the account is opened.

□□ e □□□□□□□e□□e□ t□□e □□e□ □□□□□s □□e□e□ □se□ t□ □ □□□.□□□□□
The advertisement must include the period of time during which the annual percentage yield will be offered. Alternatively, the advertisement may state that the annual percentage yield is accurate as of a specified date. The date must be recent in relation to the publication or media broadcast used for the advertisement, taking into account the particular circumstances or production deadlines involved. An advertisement may refer to the annual percentage yield as being accurate as of the date of publication, if the date is on the publication itself.

□ □□□ □□ □□□□□e □se□ t□ □ □□□.□□□□□
For accounts that have a required minimum balance, the advertisement must state the minimum balance required to obtain the advertised annual percentage yield. For tiered-rate accounts, the advertisement must state the minimum balance required for each tier in close proximity, and that statement must be as prominent as the applicable annual percentage yield.

□ □□□ □□ □□□e□□□□e□ s□t □se□ t□ □ □□□.□□□□□

For an account that requires a minimum deposit to open the account, the advertisement must state the minimum deposit required to open the account, if it is greater than the minimum balance necessary to obtain the advertised annual percentage yield.

Effect of fees (section 230.8(c))

An advertisement must state that fees could reduce the earnings on the account. This requirement only applies to maintenance or activity fees.

Features of time accounts (section 230.8(c))

For time accounts, the advertisement must include:

- Term of the account,

- Early withdrawal penalties — a statement that a penalty will or may be imposed for early withdrawal, and

- Required interest payouts — a statement that interest cannot remain on deposit and that payout of interest is mandatory for noncompounding time accounts with the following features:
  - The stated maturity is greater than one year,

  - Interest is not compounded on an annual or more frequent basis,

  - Interest is required to be paid out at least annually, and

  - The annual percentage yield is determined in accordance with section E of appendix A of Regulation DD.

Bonuses (Section 230.8(d))

If an institution states a bonus in an advertisement, the advertisement must state clearly and conspicuously the following information, if applicable to the advertised product:

- "Annual percentage yield," using that term;

- Time requirement to obtain the bonus;

- Minimum balance required to obtain the bonus;

- Minimum balance required to open the account, if it is greater than the minimum balance necessary to obtain the bonus; and

- Time when the bonus will be provided.

However, these requirements do not necessarily apply if the situation falls under the exemptions of section 230.8(e). In addition, general statements such as "bonus checking" or "get a bonus when you open a checking account" do not trigger the bonus disclosures.

Exemption for Certain Advertisements (Section 230.8(e))

Section 230.8(e) exempts certain types of media and certain indoor signs from some of the section's advertising rules.

 e e e t s se t   . e
If an institution advertises through one of the following exempted media, the advertisement is not required to include information required under certain section 230.8 rules, as outlined below:

- Broadcast or electronic media, such as television or radio. However, the exemption does not extend to Internet and email advertisements.

- Outdoor media, such as billboards.

- Telephone response machines. However, solicitations for a tiered-rate account made through telephone-response machines must provide the annual percentage yields and the balance requirements applicable to each tier.

When any of these media is used, the following advertisement requirements are exempted:

- Information required for special account features involving variable rates, time an annual percentage yield is offered, minimum opening deposit, effect of fees, and early withdrawal penalties for time accounts.

- When bonuses are advertised, information required related to a minimum balance to open an account (if it is greater than the minimum balance necessary to obtain the bonus) and when the bonus will be provided.

If an institution posts account information on signs inside its premises (or the premises of a deposit broker), the postings are exempt from the advertising requirements for:

- Permissible rates,

- When additional disclosures are required,

- Bonuses, and

- Certain exempted media.

If a sign, falling under this exemption, states a rate of return, it must:

- State the rate as an "annual percentage yield," using that term or the term "APY." The sign must not state any other rate, although the related interest rate may be stated.

- Contain a statement advising consumers to contact an employee for further information about applicable fees and terms.

Indoor signs include advertisements displayed on computer screens, banners, preprinted posters, and chalk or peg boards. Any advertisement inside the premises that can be retained by a consumer (such as a brochure or a printout from a computer) is not an indoor sign.

Additional Disclosures in Connection with the Payment of Overdrafts (Section 230.8(f))

In addition to the general requirement that advertisements not be misleading, an institution that promotes the payment of overdrafts in an advertisement must also include in the advertisement the disclosures required under section 230.11(b).

Record Retention (12 CFR 230.9)

Section 230.9(c) covers the record retention requirements in order for an institution to demonstrate compliance with Regulation DD, including rate information, advertising, and the providing of disclosures to consumers at the appropriate time (including upon a consumer's request).

Record Retention

An institution must retain records that evidence compliance for a minimum of two years after the date that disclosures are required to be made or an action is required to be taken. If required by its supervising agency, an institution may need to retain records for a longer time period.

Evidence of Required Actions

An institution may demonstrate its compliance by

- Establishing and maintaining procedures for paying interest and providing timely disclosures, and

- Retaining sample disclosures for each type of account offered to consumers such as account-opening disclosures, copies of advertisements, and change-in-term notices, as well as information regarding the interest rates and annual percentage yields offered.

Methods of Retaining Evidence

An institution must be able to reconstruct the required disclosures and other required actions, but does not need to maintain hard copies of disclosures and other records. It may keep records evidencing compliance in microfilm, microfiche, or other methods that reproduce records accurately (including computer files).

Payment of Interest

An institution must retain sufficient rate and balance information to permit the verification of interest paid on an account, including the payment of interest on the full principal balance.

Section 230.10 — [Reserved]

Additonal Disclosure Requirements for Overdraft Services (12 CFR 230.11)

Section 230.11 contains periodic statement and advertising requirements for certain discretionary overdraft services. The requirements address concerns about the uniformity and adequacy of information provided to consumers when they overdraw their deposit accounts. Specifically, they address certain types of services – sometimes referred to as "bounced-check protection" or "courtesy overdraft protection" – that institutions offer to pay consumers' checks and other items when there are insufficient funds in the account. The requirements apply to all depository institutions, regardless of whether they promote their overdraft services.

Periodic Statement Disclosures (Section 230.11(a))

Disclosure of total fees (section 230.11(a))

The institution must disclose on its periodic statements (if it provides periodic statements) separate totals for the statement period and for the calendar year to date for:

- The total dollar amount for all fees or charges imposed on the account for paying checks or other items when there are insufficient or unavailable funds and the account becomes overdrawn, using the term "Total Overdraft Fees" (the requirement to use the term "Total Overdraft Fees" is effective October 1, 2010), and

- The total dollar amount for all fees or charges imposed on the account for returning items unpaid.

The aggregate fee disclosures must be placed in close proximity to the disclosure of any fee(s) that may be imposed in connection with the account and must use a substantially similar format as shown below (see Appendix B of the regulation). The table must contain lines (or similar markings such as asterisks) inside the table to divide the columns and rows.

	Total for this period	Total year-to-date
Total Overdraft Fees	$60.00	$150.00
Total Returned Item Fees	0.00	30.00

The total dollar amount for paying overdrafts includes per-item fees as well as interest charges, daily or other periodic fees, or fees charged for maintaining an account in overdraft status, whether the overdraft is by check, debit card transaction, or by other transaction type. It also includes fees charged when there are insufficient funds because previously deposited funds are subject to a hold or are uncollected. It does not include fees for transferring funds from another account of the consumer to avoid an overdraft, or fees charged under a service subject to Regulation Z, 12 CFR 226.

The total dollar amount for all fees for returning items unpaid must include all fees charged to the account for dishonoring or returning checks or other items drawn on the account. The institution must disclose separate totals for the statement period and for the calendar year-to-date. Fees imposed when deposited items are returned are not included. Institutions may use terminology such as "returned item fee" or "NSF fee" to describe fees for returning items unpaid.

In the case of waived fees, an institution may provide a statement for the current period reflecting that fees imposed during a previous period were waived and credited to the account. Institutions may, but are not required to, reflect the adjustment in the total for the calendar year-to-date and in the applicable statement period. For example, if an institution assesses a fee in January and refunds the fee in February, the institution could disclose a year-to-date total reflecting the amount credited, but it should not affect the total disclosed for the February statement period, because the fee was not assessed in the February statement period. If an institution assesses and then waives and credits a fee within the same cycle, the institution may, at its option, reflect the adjustment in the total disclosed for fees imposed during the current statement period and for the total for the calendar year-to-date. Thus, if the institution assesses and waives the fee in the February statement period, the February fee total could reflect a total net of the waived fee.

The disclosures under this section must be included on periodic statements provided by an institution starting the first statement period that began after January 1, 2010. For example, if a consumer's statement period typically closes on the 15th of each month, an institution must provide the disclosures required by this section on subsequent periodic statements for that consumer beginning with the statement reflecting the period from January 16, 2010, to February 15, 2010.

Advertising Disclosures for Overdraft Services (Section 230.11(b))

Unless an exception in section 230.11(b)(2)-(4) applies, any advertisement promoting the payment of overdrafts must disclose in a clear and conspicuous manner all of the following:

- The fee(s) for the payment of each overdraft;

- The categories of transactions for which a fee may be imposed for paying an overdraft;

- The time period by which the consumer must repay or cover any overdraft; and

- The circumstances under which the institution will not pay an overdraft. It is sufficient to state, as applicable, "Whether your overdrafts will be paid is discretionary, and we reserve the right not to pay. For example, we typically do not pay overdrafts if your account is not in good standing, or you are not making regular deposits, or you have too many overdrafts."

The advertising disclosure rules for overdraft services do not apply in the following circumstances:

- An advertisement promoting a service for which the institution's payment of overdrafts would be agreed upon in writing and subject to Regulation Z (12 CFR 226).

- A communication by an institution about the payment of overdrafts in response to a consumer-initiated inquiry about deposit accounts or overdrafts. However, providing information about the payment of overdrafts in response to a balance inquiry made through an automated system, such as a telephone response machine, ATM, or an institution's Internet site, is not a response to a consumer-initiated inquiry that is exempt from the advertising disclosures.

- An advertisement made through broadcast or electronic media, such as television or radio. However, this exception does not apply to advertisements posted on an institution's Internet site, posted on an ATM screen, provided on telephone-response machines, or sent by electronic mail.

- An advertisement made on outdoor media, such as billboards;

- An ATM receipt;

- An in-person discussion with a consumer;

- Disclosures required by federal or other applicable law;

- Information included on a periodic statement or on a notice informing a consumer about a specific overdrawn item or the amount the account is overdrawn;

- A term in a deposit account agreement discussing the institution's right to pay overdrafts;

- A notice provided to a consumer, such as at an ATM, that completing a requested transaction may trigger a fee for overdrawing an account, or a general notice that items overdrawing an account may trigger a fee;

- Informational or educational materials concerning the payment of overdrafts if the materials do not specifically describe the institution's overdraft service; or

- An opt-out or opt-in notice regarding the institution's payment of overdrafts or provision of discretionary overdraft services.

Any advertisement made on an ATM screen or using a telephone response machine is not required to include the following:

- The categories of transactions for which a fee may be imposed for paying an overdraft, or

- The circumstances under which the institution will not pay an overdraft.

The advertising requirement to disclose fees for the payment of each overdraft does not apply to advertisements for the payment of overdrafts on indoor signs, if the indoor sign contains a clear and conspicuous statement that:

- Fees may apply, and

- Consumers should contact an employee for further information about applicable fees and terms.

An indoor sign covered under this exception is one described in section 230.8(e)(2) and the accompanying staff commentary. In addition to the staff commentary's examples of advertisements that are not considered indoor signs, an ATM screen is not considered an indoor sign for purposes of the overdraft disclosure requirements.

Balance Disclosures

In general, Section 230.11(c) covers how an institution displays a consumer's account balance information on automated systems, such as an ATM, when the institution will advance additional funds to cover insufficient or unavailable funds in a consumer's account. Specifically, if an institution discloses balance information to a consumer through an automated system, the disclosed balance may not include additional amounts that the institution may provide to cover an item when there are insufficient or unavailable funds in the consumer's account. This requirement covers additional funds that an institution may provide under a service provided at the institution's own discretion, a service subject to Regulation Z (12 CFR 226), or a service to transfer funds from another account of the consumer. However, the institution may, at its option, disclose an additional, second account balance that would include funds provided by the institution, if the institution prominently states that any such second balance includes funds that the institution may provide to cover insufficient or unavailable funds in the consumer's account and, if applicable, that additional funds are not available for all transactions.

Funds That Must Not Be Included

The balance may, but need not, include funds that are deposited in the consumer's account, such as from a check, that are not yet made available for withdrawal in accordance with the funds availability rules under Regulation CC (12 CFR 229). In addition, the balance may, but need not, include funds that are held by the institution to satisfy a prior obligation of the consumer (for example, to cover a hold for an ATM or debit card transaction that has been authorized but for which the bank has not settled).

Retail Sweep Accounts

When disclosing a transaction account balance, an institution is not required to exclude funds from the consumer's balance that may be transferred from another account pursuant to a retail sweep account. In a retail sweep program, an institution establishes two legally distinct subaccounts, a transaction subaccount and a savings subaccount. These two accounts together make up the consumer's account. Retail sweep account programs typically:

- Comply with Regulation D,

- Prevent direct access by the consumer to the non-transaction subaccount that is part of the retail sweep program, and

- Document on the consumer's periodic statements the account balance as the combined balance in the subaccounts.

Disclosing Second Balance

If an institution discloses additional balances that include funds that may be provided to cover an overdraft, the institution must prominently state that the additional balance(s) includes additional overdraft funds. The institution may not simply state, for instance, that the second balance is the consumer's "available balance," or contains "available funds." Rather, the institution should provide enough information to convey that the second balance includes funds that the institution may provide to cover insufficient or unavailable funds. For example, the institution may state that the balance includes "overdraft funds." If a consumer has not opted into (or as applicable, has opted out of) the institution's discretionary overdraft service, any additional balance disclosed should not include funds that otherwise might be available under that service. If a consumer has not opted into (or as applicable, has opted out of) the institution's discretionary overdraft service for some, but not all transactions (e.g., the consumer has not opted into overdraft services for ATM and one-time debit card transactions), an institution that includes funds from its discretionary overdraft service in the balance should convey that the overdraft funds are not available for all transactions. For example, the institution could state that overdraft funds are not available for ATM and one-time debit card transactions. Similarly, if funds are not available for all transactions pursuant to a service subject to the Board's Regulation Z (12 CFR 226) or a service that transfers funds from another account, a second balance that includes such funds should also indicate this fact.

Automated Systems

The balance disclosure requirement applies to any automated system through which the consumer requests a balance, including, but not limited to, a

---

telephone response system, the institution's Internet site, or an ATM. The requirement applies whether the institution discloses a balance through an ATM owned or operated by the institution or through an ATM not owned or operated by the institution (including an ATM operated by a nondepository institution). If the balance is obtained at an ATM, the requirement also applies whether the balance is disclosed on the ATM screen or on a paper receipt.

Effect on State Laws (Regulation DD — Appendix C)

Regulation DD preempts state law requirements that are inconsistent with the requirements of the Truth in Savings Act (TISA) or Regulation DD. A state law is inconsistent if it contradicts the definitions, disclosure requirements, or interest-calculation methods outlined in the act or the regulation. The regulation also provides that interested parties may request the board to determine whether a state law is inconsistent with the TISA.

Yield Calculations

Regulation DD's appendix A contains formulas for calculating the APY, which is stated in disclosures and advertisements for interest-bearing accounts, and the APYE, which must be disclosed on the periodic statements. The APY is an annualized rate based on a 365-day year that measures the total amount of interest paid on an account based on the interest rate and the frequency of compounding. The APYE is an annualized rate that reflects the relationship between the amount of interest actually earned on the account during an interest period and the average daily balance in the account for that period.

The APY, the APYE, and the interest rate must be rounded to the nearest 1/100 of 1 percent, and expressed to two decimal places (12 CFR 230.3(f)(1)). For account disclosures, the interest rate may be expressed to more than two decimal places. The APY and APYE have five basis points tolerance for accuracy. No tolerance exists for the interest rate (12 CFR 230.3(f)(2)).

The OCC's Annual Percentage Yield Software Program, (APYWIN 2.1), may be used by examining personnel and bankers, at their option, to verify APYs under Regulation DD (12 CFR 230) for:

- Deposit account disclosures and advertising, and

- Periodic statements.

Instructions for accessing the software are included in this booklet's appendix. This software can be downloaded free at www.occ.treas.gov/APY.htm.

Subsequent Notice Requirements for Time Accounts

Maturity	Automatically Renewable (Rollover)	Not Automatically Renewable (Non-rollover)
> One Month and > One Year	*Timing* (a) 30 calendar days before maturity, or (b) 20 calendar days before end of grace period, if a grace period is at least 5 calendar days. *Content* (a) Date existing account matures, and (b) Disclosures for a new account (§ 230.4(b)). If terms have not been determined, indicate this fact and state when they will be determined or provide a telephone number to obtain the terms. (§ 230.5(b)(1))	*Timing* 10 calendar days before maturity. *Content* Maturity date and whether or not interest will be paid after maturity. (§ 230.5(c))
> One Month and < One Year	*Timing* (a) 30 calendar days before maturity, or (b) 20 calendar days before end of grace period, if a grace period is at least 5 calendar days. *Content* (a) Disclosures required under § 230.5(b)(1), or (b) Date of maturities of existing and new accounts, any change in terms, and difference in terms between new and existing accounts. If terms have not been determined, indicate this fact and state when they will be determined or provide a telephone number to obtain the terms. (§ 230.5(b)(2))	No subsequent notice required.

Instructions for Access to APY Software (APYWIN 2.1)

You can obtain the annual percentage yield (APY) software by downloading from the OCC Web site at www.occ.treas.gov/APY.htm.

Questions about the APY computer program should be directed to the OCC's Compliance Policy Department at (202) 874-4428 or via e-mail to APYAssistance@OCC.treas.gov.

Laws

    12 USC 4301, Truth in Savings Act

Regulations

    12 CFR 230, Regulation DD

OCC Issuances

    APY Software Program (free download at www.occ.treas.gov/APY.htm)

Objective: To determine the bank's compliance with the Regulation D.

1. Select a sample of prepaid time deposits. Determine the accuracy of any interest penalty, and determine whether the penalty was calculated in accordance with disclosures provided to the depositors.

2. Review the NOW accounts trial balance or other account listing. Select a sample of NOW accounts that appear to belong to businesses (other than a sole proprietorship or an individual doing business under a trade name) and confirm eligibility. (12 CFR 204.130(c)(2), 12 USC 1832(a))

3. Determine whether the bank has implemented procedures, including the closing of accounts when necessary, to prevent more than six third-party transfers and withdrawals per calendar month from savings accounts (including MMDAs). Determine the effectiveness of the procedures by sampling "excessive transfer reports" for a reasonable number of months and any other documentation used to control excessive transfers, including, if necessary, specific deposit account statements. (12 CFR 204.2(d)(2))

4. Test the accuracy of reports of deposits filed with the Federal Reserve by reviewing the bank's supporting documentation. Further, determine whether these reports were filed on time. (12 CFR 204.3, 204.4, 204.9).

Objective: To determine the bank's compliance with the Interest on Deposits regulation.

1. Obtain and test a sample of demand deposit accounts to determine that interest is not paid on these accounts.

Expanded Procedures
Expedited Funds Availability Act

Objectives (Subparts A and B): To determine the bank's compliance with the Expedited Funds Availability Act.

Determine that the financial institution has established internal controls for compliance with Regulation CC's provisions relating to funds availability.

Determine that the financial institution has established a training program for applicable employees addressing Regulation CC responsibilities.

Determine that the financial institution maintains records of compliance with Regulation CC for a period of two years.

[Note: Subpart C of Regulation CC, "Collection of Checks," has been omitted. It addresses exclusively payment systems issues among financial institutions. Subpart C does not have consumer-related regulatory compliance issues to examine.]

1. Determine the types of transaction accounts, as defined in Regulation D [section 204.2(e)] (e.g., demand deposits, NOW accounts, ATS accounts) offered by the financial institution.

2. Obtain copies of the forms used by the financial institution for transaction accounts, including, but not limited to, the following:

    *   Specific availability policy disclosures
    *   Exception hold notices
    *   Case-by-case hold notices
    *   Special deposit slips
    *   Change in terms notices

3. Determine, by account type, the institution's specific funds availability policies with regard to deposits.

4. Determine which employees perform the various activities necessary to comply with the different provisions of Regulation CC. This would include, for example, personnel engaged in

- Distributing disclosure statements.
- Employee training.
- Internal reviews.
- Computer program development for deposit accounts (not necessarily a computer programmer).
- Deposit operations.
- Overdraft administration.
- ATM deposit processing.
- Private (personal) banking.
- Determining case-by-case holds or exceptions.

5. Review the financial institution's training manual, internal audit or similar reports for Regulation CC, written procedures given to employees detailing their responsibilities under the regulation, and other similar materials.

6. Determine the extent and adequacy of the instruction and training received by the employees listed above to enable them to carry out their assigned responsibilities under Regulation CC.

7. Verify that the institution provides employees with a written copy of the Regulation CC procedures corresponding to their area of responsibility. [12 CFR 229.19(f)]

Expedited Funds Availability Act Checklist

This checklist can be used for reviewing audit work papers, evaluating bank policies, performing transaction testing, and training as appropriate. Complete only those aspects of the checklist that specifically relate to the issue being reviewed, evaluated or tested, and retain those completed sections in the work papers.

When reviewing audit or evaluating bank policies, a "No" answer indicates a possible exception/deficiency and should be explained in the work papers. When performing transaction testing, a "No" answer indicates a possible violation and should be explained in the work papers. If a line item is not applicable within the area you are reviewing, just indicate "NA."

Underline the applicable use: Audit   Bank Policies   Transaction Testing

Subpart B — Availability of Funds and Disclosure of Funds Availability Policies

	YES	NO
Date of Deposit		
1. Does the bank consider every day except Saturday, Sunday, and federal holidays, as a "business day"? If 1/1, 7/4, 11/11 or 12/25 fall on a Saturday, the previous Friday is a business day even though it is a federal holiday. [12 CFR 229.2(g)]		
2. Does the bank consider as a "banking day" that part of any business day during which an office of the bank is open for substantially all of its business? [12 CFR 229.2(f)]		
3. Does the bank have a cut-off, for receipt of deposits, of 2 p.m. or later for bank offices and noon or later for ATMs? [12 CFR 229.19(a)(5)(ii)]		
4. Does the bank comply with the following rules in determining when funds are considered to have been deposited? <ul><li>Deposits over the counter or at ATMs are considered deposited when "received." [12 CFR 229.19(a)(1)]</li><li>Mail deposits are considered deposited when they are received by the mailroom of the bank. [12 CFR 229.19(a)(2) and commentary]</li><li>Deposits in a night depository, lock box, or similar facility are considered received when the deposits are removed from the facility and are available for processing. [12 CFR 229.19(a)(3)]</li><li>Deposits at an off-premises ATM (not within 50 feet of the bank) that is not serviced more than twice a week are considered received as of the date the deposits are removed from the ATM by the bank. [12 CFR 229.19(a)(4)]</li><li>Deposits made on a nonbanking day are considered to have been received no later than the next banking day. [12 CFR 229.19(a)(5)(i)]</li><li>When funds must be available on a given "business day," the bank makes the funds available at the later of 9 a.m. or at the time the bank's teller facilities (including ATMs) are available for account withdrawals. [12 CFR 229.19(b)]</li><li>If the bank limits cash withdrawals, the bank makes $400 available for cash withdrawals no later than 5 p.m. on the appropriate business day (second day for local checks, fifth for nonlocal checks) following the day of deposit. [12 CFR 229.12(d)]</li></ul>		

Required Next Day Availability		
5. Does the bank make funds from the following types of deposits available for withdrawal no later than the first business day following the date of deposit: • Electronic payments. [12 CFR 229.10(b)] • Checks drawn on the U.S. Treasury and deposited to the payee's account. [12 CFR 229.10(c)(1)(i)] • "On Us" checks or checks that are drawn on and deposited in branches of the same bank in the same state or check processing region. [12 CFR 229.10(c)(1)(vi)]		

6. Does the bank make funds from the following deposits available no later than the first business day after the day of deposit, if the deposit is made in person to a bank employee, or no later than the second business day if the deposit is not made in person to a bank employee?
• Cash deposits. [12 CFR 229.10(a)(1) and (2)]
• U.S. Postal Service money orders deposited in an account held by the payee of the check. [12 CFR 29.10(c)(1)(ii), 12 CFR 229.10(c)(2)]
• Checks drawn on a Federal Reserve Bank or Federal Home Loan Bank deposited in an account held by the payee of the check. [12 CFR 229.10(c)(1)(iii), 12 CFR 229.10(c)(2)]
• Checks drawn by a state or local governmental unit and deposited:
  – In an account held by the payee of the check [12 CFR 229.10(c)(1)(iv)(A), 12 CFR 229.10(c)(2)]
  – In a depositary bank located in the same state as the governmental unit issuing the check [12 CFR 229.10(c)(1)(iv)(B), 12 CFR 229.10(c)(2)]; and
  – Accompanied by a special deposit slip (if required by the bank to make the funds available on the next business day). [12 CFR 229.10(c)(1)(iv)(D), 12 CFR 229.10(c)(3)]
• Cashier's checks, certified checks, and teller's checks (as defined in 12 CFR 229.2) deposited in an account held by the payee of the check when the check is accompanied by a special deposit slip (if required by the bank).
   [12 CFR 229.10(c)(1)(v)(C), 229.10(c)(3)]		

7. Are the special deposit slips reasonably available? [12 CFR 229.10(c)(3)(ii)]		
8. When checks not subject to the next-day availability rules are deposited, does the bank make available the lesser of $100 or the amount deposited to all the customer's accounts? [12 CFR 229.10(c)(1)(vii)]		
Local Checks and Certain Other Deposits		
10. Are funds from local checks generally available no later than the second business day after the day of deposit? [12 CFR 229.12(b)(1)]		
11. If the bank extends by one business day the time period for which deposits subject to 12 CFR 229.12(b), (c), or (f) are made available: [12 CFR 229.12(d)] • Is $100 available for withdrawal in cash or by check on the next business day after the day of deposit as required by 229.10(c)(1)(vii)? • Is an additional $400 available for cash withdrawal by 5:00 pm on the business day specified in 12 CRR 229.12(b), (c), or (f)? • Are any remaining funds available for withdrawal the business day following the business day specified in 229.12(b), (c), or (f) after the $400 was made available? NOTE: The rule does not supersede the bank's cash withdrawal limits.		

12. For Treasury checks; U.S. Postal Service money orders; checks drawn on the Federal Reserve; Federal Home Loan Bank checks; state or local government checks; or cashier's, certified, and teller's checks that do not meet the criteria for next-day availability, does the bank make funds available no later than the second business day after the date of deposit? [12 CFR 229.12(b)(2), (3), and (4)]		
13. Are funds deposited by cash or check at a nonproprietary ATM available no later than the fifth business day after the banking day of deposit? [12 CFR 229.12(f)]		

Nonlocal Checks		
14. Are funds from nonlocal checks generally available no later than the fifth business day after the day of deposit? [12 CFR 229.12(c)(1)]		
15. If the bank is located in a check processing territory listed in appendix B-2, does it have procedures to make funds for certain nonlocal checks available not later than the times specified in that appendix? [12 CFR 229.12(c)(2)]		

Payable Through Checks		
16. If local and nonlocal checks are treated differently, • Does the bank's specific availability policy disclosure state that payable-through checks will be treated as local or nonlocal based on the location of the bank where the check is payable? [12 CFR 229.16(b)(2) and footnote 1] • Does the bank's specific availability policy disclosure either: – Describe how the customer can determine whether the checks will be treated as local or nonlocal, or – State that special rules apply and that the customer may ask about the availability of these checks? [12 CFR 229.16(b)(2), footnote 1]		

Extended Holds (Case-by-Case Holds)		
17. Does the bank's specific availability policy disclosures indicate that case-by-case holds may be placed? [12 CFR 229.16(c)(1)] If yes, does the disclosure: • State that the bank may extend the period for which deposits are unavailable for withdrawal? [12 CFR 229.16(c)(1)(i)] • Provide the latest time a deposit will be available for withdrawal if the period of unavailability is extended? [12 CFR 229.16(c)(1)(i)] • State that the bank will notify the customer if funds from a particular deposit will exceed the time period outlined in the bank's funds availability policy? [12 CFR 229.16(c)(1)(ii)] • Encourage customers to ask when particular deposits will be made available for withdrawal? [12 CFR 229.16(c)(1)(iii)]		
18. When case-by-case holds are placed, does the bank provide the customer with a written notice of the hold? [12 CFR 229.16(c)(2)]		
19. Does the notice include: • The customer's account number? [12 CFR 229.16(c)(2)(i)(A)] • The date of the deposit? [12 CFR 229.16(c)(2)(i)(B)] • The amount of the deposit that is being delayed? [12 CFR 229.16(c)(2)(i)(C)] • The day the funds will be available for withdrawal? [12 CFR 229.16(c)(2)(i)(D)]		
20. Does the bank provide the notice at the time the deposit is made, if the deposit is made to an employee of the depositary bank? [12 CFR 229.16(c)(2)(ii)]		
21. If the notice is not given at the time of deposit, does the depositary bank mail or deliver the notice to the customer not later than the first business day after the day of the deposit? [12 CFR 229.16(c)(2)(ii)]		

22. If the bank does not provide the notice at the time of deposit, does it refrain from charging the customer overdraft or return check fees if:
   • The overdraft or other fee would not have occurred if the deposited check had not been delayed, and
   • The deposited check was paid by the paying bank? [12 CFR 229.16(c)(3)]		

23. If the bank does not provide the notice at the time of deposit and charges overdraft fees, does it notify the customer of the right to a refund of such fees and how to obtain the refund? [12 CFR 229.16(c)(3)]		
24. Does the bank refund the fees if the conditions listed in question 23 are met and the customer requests a refund? [12 CFR 229.16(c)(3)]		
Exception-Based Holds		

25. When invoking an exception hold for other than new accounts, does the bank provide the customer with a written notice that includes:
   • The customer's account number? [12 CFR 229.13(g)(1)(i)(A)]
   • The date of the deposit? [12 CFR 229.13(g)(1)(i)(B)]
   • The amount of the deposit that is being delayed? [12 CFR 229.13(g)(1)(i)(C)]
   • The reason the exception was invoked? [12 CFR 229.13(g)(1)(i)(D)]
   • The day the funds will be available for withdrawal (unless the emergency conditions exception is invoked and the bank does not know when the funds will become available)? [12 CFR 229.13(g)(1)(i)(E)] [12 CFR 229.13(g)(4)]		

26. Does the bank refrain from delaying funds availability beyond a reasonable time period? [12 CFR 229.13(h)] **NOTE:** An extension of up to five days for local checks and six days for nonlocal checks is considered reasonable.		
Exceptions		
New Accounts [12 CFR 229.13(a)]		
27. Does the bank's definition of a new account comply with the definition under 12 CFR 229.13(a)(2)? **NOTE:** If a customer has had another transaction account at the bank within the 30 days before opening an account, the customer does not qualify for the "new account" exception.		
28. If the bank's definition is different, does it delay availability to new account holders beyond the limits set forth in the regulation?		
29. Do bank disclosures accurately reflect the bank's practice for making deposited funds available for new accounts? [12 CFR 229.16(b)(3)]		
30. Do cash deposits made in person to a bank employee become available for withdrawal on the first business day following the day of deposit? [12 CFR 229.13(a)(1)(i), 12 CR 229.10(a)(1)]		
31. Are cash deposits not made in person to a bank employee available for withdrawal on the second business day following the day of deposit? [12 CFR 229.13(a)(1)(i), 12 CFR 229.10(a)(2)]		
32. Are electronic transfers into new accounts available for withdrawal on the business day following the day the transfer is received? [12 CFR 229.13(a)(1)(i), 229.10(b)]		

33. Is the first $5,000 from any of the following types of check deposits available for withdrawal from a new account not later than the first business day after the day of the deposit, if the deposits meet the requirements of section 229.10(c)* [12 CFR 229.13(a)(1)(ii)]: • Treasury checks? [12 CFR 229.10(c)(1)(i)] • U.S. Postal Service money orders? [12 CFR 229.10(c)(1)(ii)] • Federal Reserve or Federal Home Loan Bank checks? [12 CFR 229.10(c)(1)(iii)] • State or local government checks? [12 CFR 229.10(c)(1)(iv)] • Cashier's, certified, and teller's checks? [12 CFR 229.10(c)(1)(v)] * See checklist item on next-day availability and Introduction Subpart 8, Availability Policy.		
34. Is the amount of any deposit type listed in question #33 exceeding $5,000 available for withdrawal no later than the ninth business day following the day of deposit accounts? [12 CFR 229.13(a)(1)(ii)]		

Large Deposits [12 CFR 229.13(b)]		
35. If the bank invokes the large deposit rule, does it do so only to that portion of the aggregate local and nonlocal check deposits, which exceed $5,000 on any one banking day? [12 CFR 229.13(b)]		
36. Does the bank refrain from applying this exception to deposits made in cash, to deposits by electronic payment, or to checks that must receive next-day availability under section 12 CFR 229.10(c)? **NOTE:** See commentary to section 229.13(b)-1		
37. Does the bank provide customers with a written notice of the longer delay? [12 CFR 229.13(g)(1)] Is the notice: • Provided at the time of the deposit, when the deposit is received in person by an employee of the bank, or • Mailed on or before the first business day after the day the bank learns of the facts giving rise to the exception?		

Redeposited Checks [12 CFR 229.13(c)]		
38. Does the bank refrain from applying the redeposited exception to: • Checks that are returned because of a missing endorsement and are subsequently indorsed and redeposited? [12 CFR 229.13(c)(1)] • Checks which were returned because they were postdated, but are not postdated when redeposited? [12 CFR 229.13(c)(2)]		
39. Does the bank consider the day the check was redeposited to be the day of deposit when determining when funds must be made available for withdrawal? [See commentary to 12 CFR 229.13(c)]		

Repeated Overdrafts [12 CFR 229.13(d)]		
40. Are exception holds articulated in the bank's specific availability policy disclosure statement? [12 CFR 229.16(a)]		
41. Does the bank invoke the repeated overdraft exception only when the account balance is negative (or would have been negative had checks or other charges been paid): • On six or more days during the preceding six months [12 CFR 229.13(d)(1)], or • On two or more days during the preceding six months, if the amount of any negative balance would have been $5,000 or more? [12 CFR 229.13(d)(2)]		
42. Does the bank impose longer holds for depositors who have a history of overdrafts?		

43. When the bank imposes the longer delay period, is the depositor notified of the reason, in writing, at the time of deposit? If not, is a notice mailed on or before the first business day after the day of the deposit or the day the bank learns the facts giving rise to the exception? [12 CFR 229.13(g)]		
44. Does the bank return the account to the normal availability schedule when the account is no longer repeatedly overdrawn? [12 CFR 229.13(d)] NOTE: Banks may use this exception for six months after the last overdraft that makes the depositor a "repeated overdraft."		
Reasonable Cause to Doubt Collectibility [12 CFR 229.13(e)]		
45. When the bank invokes a reasonable cause exception, does it provide the customer with a written notice of exception at the time the deposit was made, if the deposit was made in person to an employee of the bank? [12 CFR 229.13(g)(1)(ii)]		
46. If the deposit was not made in person to an employee of the bank, or if the hold was placed because of information learned subsequent to the receipt of the deposit, does the bank mail the exception notice to the customer? [12 CFR 229.13(g)(1)(ii)]		
47. Does the bank retain copies of each reasonable cause exception notice, along with a brief statement of the facts that lead to the hold, for a period of two years? [12 CFR 229.13(g)(5)]		
48. Does the bank refrain from invoking the reasonable cause exception based on the class of the depositor or the check? [12 CFR 229.13(e)(1)]		
49. Does the bank refrain from assessing a fee for any subsequent overdraft, returned check, or other unpaid charge (or advise customers of their right to a refund of such fees and refund them on request) if all of the following are met: • The depositary bank extended the period of unavailability because the check was deemed uncollectible [12 CFR 229.13(e)(1)]; • The depositor was not provided with the written notice required by section 229.13(g)(1) at time of deposit [12 CFR 229.13(e)(2)]; • The overdraft or return would not have occurred if the availability period had not been extended [12 CFR 229.13(e)(2)(i)]; and • The deposited check was finally paid by the paying bank? [12 CFR 229.13(e)(2)(ii)]		
50. Does the exception notice inform the customer where to direct a request for a refund of the overdraft fees? [12 CFR 229.13(e)(2))		
Emergency Conditions [12 CFR 229.13(f)]		
51. Does the bank invoke the emergency conditions exception only in the following circumstances and when the bank has exercised necessary diligence as circumstances require: • An interruption of communications or computer or other equipment [12 CFR 229.13(f)(1)], • Suspension of payments by another bank [12 CFR 229.13(f)(2)], • War [12 CFR 229.13(f)(3)], or • Other emergency condition beyond the control of the bank? [12 CFR 229.13(f)(4)]		
52. Does the bank make funds available for withdrawal no later than a reasonable period after the emergency has ended or within the time period established by the temporary and permanent schedules, whichever is later? [12 CFR 229.13(h)(3)] NOTE: As stated in 12 CFR 229.13(h)(4), a reasonable period is an extension of up to five business days for local checks and six days for nonlocal checks.		

53. Does the bank provide customers with a written notice of the longer delay? [12 CFR 229.13(g)(1)]		
54. Is the notice provided at the time of the deposit, if the deposit is received in person by an employee of the bank or is the notice mailed on or before the first business day after the day the bank learns of the facts giving rise to the exception? [12 CFR 229.13(g)(1)(ii)]		
Miscellaneous		
55. Does the bank provide employees with a written statement regarding the bank's procedures for expedited funds availability that pertain to that employee's function? [12 CFR 229.19(f)]		
56. Does the bank calculate funds availability for nonconsumer accounts based on the customer's typical deposit mix? If yes, obtain a copy of the bank's formula for determining its availability schedule. Review a sample of checks* similar to that used by the bank to calculate funds availability and answer the following [12 CFR 229.19(d)]: • Does the formula accurately represent the average composition of the customer's deposits? • Does the specified percentage of available funds appear reasonable? (Is a set percentage available the next business day, with remaining funds available according to the customer's deposit mix?) • Are the terms of availability for the account equivalent to or more prompt than the terms of availability required by the regulation? • * Select a large corporate account subject to the formula. Ask the bank to demonstrate how funds are made available to the customer. Determine whether it appears that the formula accurately reflects the type of deposit mix reasonably expected for this type of account holder. For example, a local grocery store may have 90 percent of its deposits made up of local check deposits. Therefore, a formula providing a deposit mix of at least 90 percent availability within two days may be reasonable. A mail order firm, on the other hand, may have a large percent of nonlocal checks in its check deposits. Therefore, its formula may allow for lengthier availability schedules.		
57. Does the bank display a notice of its availability policy in a conspicuous place at locations where employees receive consumer deposits? [12 CFR 229.18(b)] **NOTE:** Drive-up windows, night depositories, and locations where deposits are not taken do not require the notice. See commentary to 12 CFR 229.18(b).		
58. Does the bank display a notice at each of its proprietary ATMs stating that the funds deposited in the ATM may not be available for immediate withdrawal? [12 CFR 229.18(c)(1)]		
59. If the bank has off-premise ATMs from which funds are not collected more than twice a week, does the bank disclose, on or at the ATM, the days on which the deposits made at the ATM will be considered "received"? [12 CFR 229.18(c)(2)]		
60. Does the bank include a notice on all preprinted deposit slips that the deposited funds may not be available for immediate withdrawal? [12 CFR 229.18(a)]		

Payment of Interest		
61. Review a copy of the bank's availability schedule for check deposits credited through the Reserve Bank or its correspondent bank. Determine the time that the bank receives provisional credit for check deposits. Also determine the following: • For each interest-bearing transaction account offered by the bank (e.g., NOW accounts, ATS accounts), does the bank begin to accrue interest on the funds deposited no later than the business day on which the bank receives credit for the funds? [12 CFR 229.14] • If the bank pays interest as of the date provisional credit is granted, review the bank's schedule for provisional credit. (This schedule may be from a Federal Reserve Bank or may be based on the time credit is generally received from a correspondent bank.) Select a NOW account statement and ask the bank to detail the interest rate calculation. Select another NOW account statement and verify that the bank accrues interest as of the date provisional credit is received.		

Institutions Located Outside the Continental U.S.		
62. For offices located in Alaska, Hawaii, Puerto Rico and the U.S. Virgin Islands does the bank extend availability for check deposits drawn on banks in other states? If yes, • Is the extension limited to checks drawn on banks in a different state? (A Hawaiian bank could receive a "local" check drawn on a bank in Honolulu or a bank in San Francisco. Only the San Francisco check can be delayed.) [12 CFR 229.12 (e)]		

Subpart D — Substitute Checks
General Provisions [12 CFR 229.51 and 229.52]

63. If a bank has received consideration for a substitute check (including a paper or electronic representation) that it transfers, presents, or returns, • Does the substitute check accurately represent all of the information on the front and back of the original check as of the time the check was truncated? [12 CFR 229.51(a)(1)] • Does the substitute check bear the legend, "This is a legal copy of your check. You can use it the same way you would use the original check"? [12 CFR 229.51(a)(2)] • Will neither the depositary bank, the drawee, the drawer, or the endorser be charged for or asked to make a payment on the check (because it was already paid)? [12 CFR 229.52(a)(2)]		
64. Does the bank serve as a reconverting bank as defined in 12 CFR 229.2(zz)? If so, do the substitute checks: • Bear all endorsements applied by parties that previously handled the check, in any form for forward collection or return? [12 CFR 229.51(b)(1)]; • Identify the reconverting bank in a manner that preserves any previous reconverting bank's identifications, in accordance with ANS X9.100-140 and appendix D of 12 CFR 229? [12 CFR 229.51(b)(2)]; • Identify the bank that truncated the original check, in accordance with ANS X9.100-140 and appendix D of 12 CFR 229? [12 CFR 229.51(b)(3)]		

Expedited Recredit for Consumers [12 CFR 229.54]		
65. Has the bank had any re-credit claims under 12 CFR 229.54? If so: • Did the bank receive the claim by the end of the 40th calendar day after the delivery of the periodic statement [12 CFR 229.54(b)(1)(i)(A)] or when the substitute check giving rise to the claim was delivered? [12 CFR 229.54(b)(1)(i)(B)] • Does the bank extend the timing requirements for submission of a claim in extenuating circumstances and for an additional reasonable amount of time? [12 CFR 229.54(b)(1)(ii)] • If the bank requires the claim to be in writing and the attempt for submission was oral, does the bank inform the customer of the written requirement and provide an additional 10 days for submission of a claim? [12 CFR 229.54(b)(1)(iii)] and [12 CFR 229.54(b)(3)(ii)]		
66. Does the bank's policy permit additional time, beyond the regulatory required minimums, for submission of claims?		
67. Did the claim contain a description of the claim, a statement and estimate of loss, the reason why the original check or a sufficient copy is necessary, and sufficient information for the bank to investigate? [12 CFR 229.54(b)(2)(i)] • If the claim did not contain the required information, did the bank inform the consumer that the claim was not complete and identify what information was missing? [12 CFR 229.54(b)(2)(ii)]		
68. If a claim is received in a timely manner and the bank determines the claim to be valid: • Did the bank re-credit the consumer's account up to the substitute check amount, plus interest if the account is an interest-bearing account, no later than the end of the business day after receiving determination? [12 CFR 229.54(c)(1)(i)] • Did the bank send to the consumer a notice as required by 12 CFR 229.54(e)(1) no later than the business day following the banking day on which the bank recredits the account? [12 CFR 229.54(c)(1)(ii)]		
69. Does the notice describe: • The amount of the recredit? [12 CFR 229.54(e)(1)(i)] • The date on which the recredited funds will be available for withdrawal? [12 CFR 229.54(e)(1)(ii)]		
70. If the bank determines the claim by the consumer to be invalid, does the bank send a notice as required by 12 CFR 229.54(e)(2) no later than the business day following the banking day on which the banks makes its determination? [12 CFR 229.54 (c)(2)]		
71 Does the notice: • Include the original check or a sufficient copy, except as provided in 12 CFR 229.58; [12 CFR 229.54(e)(2)(i)] • Demonstrate to the consumer that the substitute check was properly charged or the consumer's warranty claim is not valid; [12 CFR 229.54(e)(2)(ii)] • Include the information or documents (in addition to the original check or sufficient copy), if any, on which the bank relied in making its determination or a statement that the consumer may request copies of such information or documents? [12 CFR 229.54(e)(2)(iii)]		

72. If the bank has not taken any action as required by paragraph (c)(1) or (c)(2), before the end of the 10th business day after receiving a claim, did the bank:
 • Recredit the consumer's account for the amount of loss up to $2,500, plus interest if the account is interest bearing? [12 CFR 229.54(c)(3)(i)(A)]
 • Send the consumer a notice that describes:
   – The amount of the recredit and
   – The date on which the recredited funds will be available for withdrawal? [12 CFR 229.54(e)(1)] and [12 CFR 229.54(c)(3)(i)(B)]		

73. If at the end of the 45th calendar day after the banking day on which the bank received the claim and sent to the consumer the notice the bank has still not determined if the claim is valid or invalid, did the bank [12 CFR 229.54(c)(3)(ii)]
 • Recredit the consumer's account for the remaining amount of the consumer's loss, if any, up to the amount of the substitute check, plus interest if the account is an interest-bearing account?
 • Send a notice that describes
   – The amount of the recredit and
   – The date on which the recredited funds will be available for withdrawal? [12 CFR 229.54(e)(1)] and [12 CFR 229.54(c)(3)(ii)]		

74. If the bank reverses a recredit because it later determined the claim to be invalid: [12 CFR 229.54(c)(4)(i)]
 • Did the bank notify the consumer no later than the business day after the banking day on which the bank made the reversal? [12 CFR 229.54(e)(3)]
 [12 CFR 229.54(c)(4)(ii)]
 • Did the notice:
   – Include the original check or a sufficient copy, except as provided in 12 CFR 229.58? [12 CFR 229.54(e)(2)(i)]
   – Demonstrate to the consumer that the substitute check was properly charged or that the consumer's warranty claim is not valid? [12 CFR 229.54(e)(2)(ii)]
   – Include the information or documents (in addition to the original check or sufficient copy), if any, on which the bank relied in making its determination or a statement that the consumer may request copies of such information or documents? [12 CFR 229.54(e)(2)(iii)]
   – Include the amount of the reversal, including both the amount of the recredit (including the interest component, if any) and the amount of interest paid on the recredited amount, if any, being reversed? [12 CFR 229.54(e)(3)(i)]
   – Include the date on which the bank made the reversal?
 [12 CFR 229.54(e)(3)(ii)]		

75. Does the bank make any amount that it recredits to a consumer account available for withdrawal no later than the start of the business day after the banking day on which the bank provides the recredit? [12 CFR 229.54(d)(1)] If not, • Did the bank invoke its right to delay immediate availability of recredited funds because of (1) new account status, (2) overdrawn account status, or (3) well-reasoned suspicion of fraud? [12 CFR 229.54(d)(2)] • Were the funds made available no later than the business day after the banking day on which the final determination was made **OR** the 45th calendar day after the bank received the claim, whichever occurred first? [12 CFR 229.54(d)(2)]		
76. If the bank invoked its right to delay immediate availability of recredited funds, did it refrain from imposing an overdraft fee the until the fifth calendar day after the calendar day on which the bank sent the notice of recredit? [12 CFR 229.54(d)(3)]		

Consumer Awareness [12 CFR 229.57]		
77. Did the bank disclose to its customers who receive paid checks with their statements the notice required no later than the first regularly scheduled communication after October 28, 2004? [12 CFR 229.57 (b)(1)(i)]		
78. Does the bank provide the required disclosure at the time a customer relationship is established after October 28, 2004? [12 CFR 229.57(b)(1)(ii)]		
79. Does the notice describe: • That a substitute check is the legal equivalent of an original check; [12 CFR 229.57(a)(1)] and • The consumer's recredit rights that apply when a consumer in good faith believes that a substitute check was not properly charged to his or her account? [12 CFR 229.57(a)(2)] Note that Model For C-5A Substitute Check Policy Disclosure provides a safe harbor for the content requirements provided that the bank's policies and procedures are consistent with the disclosure.		
80. Does the bank provide notice to at least one customer on jointly held accounts? [12 CFR 229.57(b)(3)]		
81. Does the bank provide the disclosure to a customer who requested an original check or a copy of a check and received a substitute check in response? [12 CFR 229.57(b)(2)(i)] If so, • Does the bank provide this disclosure at the time of the consumer's request, if feasible, or • Does the bank provide this disclosure no later than the time at which the bank provides a substitute check in response to the consumer's request?		
82. Does the bank provide the disclosure to a customer who receives a returned substitute check (at the time the bank provides such substitute check)? [12 CFR 229.57(b)(2)(ii)]		
83. Does the bank provide the required disclosures or, as necessary, an original check or a sufficient copy by U.S. mail or by other means the recipient has agreed to? [12 CFR 229.58]		

Objective: To determine the bank's compliance with the Truth in Savings Act.

Using the requested material provided by the bank:

1. Determine that account disclosure information is provided to new or potential deposit account customers within the appropriate time frames.

2. Determine whether account disclosures for each type of deposit account are accurate and provided in a timely manner.

3. Determine whether the subsequent disclosures (12 CFR 230.5, Change in Terms and Prematurity Disclosures for Time Accounts) are accurate and policies and procedures governing these disclosures are satisfactory.

4. Verify the accuracy of the periodic statement disclosures.

5. Determine that the bank's method of calculating interest is acceptable.

6. If the account disclosures do not include a statement that accrued but uncredited interest will be forfeited if the customer closes the account, verify that the accrued interest is paid when the account is closed.

7. Determine that the bank's advertising and its governing policies are consistent with the regulatory requirements.

Truth in Savings Checklist

This checklist can be used to review audit work papers, to evaluate financial institution policies, to perform transaction testing, and to train as appropriate. Complete only those aspects of the checklist that specifically relate to the issue being reviewed, evaluated, or tested, and retain those completed sections in the work papers.

When reviewing audit or evaluating financial institution policies, a "No" answer indicates a possible exception/deficiency and should be explained in the work papers. When performing transaction testing, a "No" answer indicates a possible violation and should be explained in the work papers. If a line item is not applicable within the area you are reviewing, indicate by using "NA."

Underline the applicable use: Audit   Financial institution Policies   Transaction Testing

Regulation DD — Truth In Savings Examination Checklist	Yes	No	NA
Section 230.3 — General Disclosure Requirements			
1. Does the institution make the required disclosures clearly and conspicuously in writing and in a form the consumer may keep? (§ 230.3(a))			
2. If the disclosures are combined with other account disclosures, is it clear which disclosures are applicable to the consumer's account? (§ 230.3(a))			
3. If the institution provides disclosures to a consumer in electronic form, does the institution obtain the consumer's consent, if required, and comply with the other applicable provisions of the Electronic Signatures in Global and National Commerce Act (E-Sign Act) (15 USC 7001 et seq.)? (§ 230.3(a))			
4. Do the disclosures reflect the terms of the legal obligation of the account agreement between the consumer and the institution? (§ 230.3(b))			
5. If the disclosures are provided in a language other than English, are disclosures also available in English upon request? (§ 230.3(b))			
6. Do the disclosures use consistent terminology when describing terms or features that are required to be disclosed? (staff commentary § 230.3(a)-2)			
7. Does the institution substitute disclosures required by Regulation E for disclosures required by this regulation? (§ 230.3(c))			
8. Does the institution provide disclosures to at least one account holder if there are multiple holders? (§ 230.3(d))			

Regulation DD — Truth In Savings
Examination Checklist

	Yes	No	NA
9. Do the institution's oral responses to a consumer's inquiry about interest rates payable on accounts state the annual percentage yield (APY)? If the institution chooses, it may state the interest rate, but no other rate. (§ 230.3(e))			
10. Are the APY, annual percentage yield earned (APYE), and the interest rate rounded to the nearest one-hundredth of one percentage point (0.01%) and expressed to two decimal places? (§ 230.3(f)(1))			
• For account disclosures, is the interest rate expressed to two or more decimal places? (§ 230.3(f)(1))			
11. Are the APY and APYE not more than one-twentieth of one percentage point (0.05%) above or below the APY and APYE determined in accordance with appendix A of Regulation DD? (§ 230.3(f)(2))			
Section 230.4 — Account Disclosures			
Delivery of Account Disclosures			
Account Opening			
1. Does the institution provide initial disclosures before an account is opened or a service provided, whichever is earlier? (§ 230.4(a)(1)(i))			
• If the consumer is not present when the account is open or a service is provided (and has not already received the disclosures), does the institution mail or deliver the disclosures no later than 10 business days after the account is opened or the service is provided, whichever is earlier? (§ 230.4(a)(1)(i))			
If the consumer who is not present at the institution uses electronic means to open an account or to request a service, are the disclosures provided before the account is open or the service is provided? (§ 230.4(a)(1)(ii))			
Consumer Request			
2. Does the institution have full account disclosures, including complete fee schedules, available to be provided to consumers upon request? This requirement pertains to all consumer requests, whether or not the consumer is an existing customer or a prospective customer. (§ 230.4(a)(2)(i))			
• If the consumer makes the request in person, does the institution have disclosures available to be provided upon request?			
• If the consumer who is not present at the institution makes a request, does the institution mail or deliver the account disclosures within a reasonable time after it receives the request (generally no more than 10 days)? (§ 230.4(a)(2)(i))			
3. In providing disclosures upon request, does the institution choose one of the following options when providing rate information: (§ 230.4(a)(2)(ii))			
• Specify an interest rate and APY that were offered within the most recent seven calendar days? (§ 230.4(a)(2)(ii)(A))			

Regulation DD — Truth In Savings Examination Checklist	Yes	No	NA
• State that the rate and yield are accurate as of an identified date? (§ 230.4(a)(2)(ii)(A)) **OR**			
• Provide a telephone number that consumers may call to obtain current rate information? (§ 230.4(a)(2)(ii)(A))			
4. For a time deposit account, does the institution choose to state the maturity of the time account as a term rather than a date? (§ 230.4(a)(2)(ii)(B))			
Content of Disclosures			
Rate Information			
5. Do account disclosures include, as applicable: (§ 230.4(b))			
• The "annual percentage yield" and interest rate, using those terms? (§ 230.4(b)(1(i))			
• For fixed-rate accounts, the period of time the interest rate will be in effect? (§ 230.4(b)(1)(i))			
6. For variable-rate accounts, do account disclosures include the following information: (§ 230.4(b)(1)(ii))			
• The fact that the interest rate and APY may change? (§ 230.4(b)(1)(ii)(A))			
• How the interest rate is determined? (§ 230.4(b)(1)(ii)(B))			
• The frequency with which the interest rate may change? (§ 230.4(b)(1)(ii)(C)) **AND**			
• Any limit on the amount the interest rate may change? (§ 230.4(b)(1)(ii)(D))			
Compounding and Crediting			
7. Do the account disclosures describe the frequency with which interest is compounded and credited? (§ 230.4(b)(2)(i))			
8. If consumers will forfeit interest if they close the account before accrued interest is credited, do the account disclosures include a statement that interest will not be paid in such cases? (§ 230.4(b)(2)(ii))			
Balance Information			
9. As applicable, do the account disclosures: (§ 230.4(b)(3)(i))			
• Describe the minimum balance required to:			
– Open an account? (§ 230.4(b)(3)(i)(A))			
– Avoid the imposition of a fee? (§ 230.4(b)(3)(i)(B))			
– Obtain the APY disclosed? (§ 230.4(b)(3)(i)(C))			
• Describe how the minimum balance requirement is determined to avoid the imposition of a fee or to obtain the APY disclosed? (§ 230.4(b)(3)(i))			
• Explain the balance computation method used to calculate interest on the account? (§ 230.4(b)(3)(ii))			
• State when interest begins to accrue on noncash deposits? (§ 230.4(b)(3)(iii))			

Regulation DD — Truth In Savings Examination Checklist	Yes	No	NA
Fees			
Do the account disclosures state the amount of any fee that may be imposed in connection with the account (or an explanation of how the fee will be determined) and the conditions under which the fee may be imposed? (§ 230.4(b)(4))			
• Regardless of whether the institution promotes overdraft payment, does it disclose specific categories of transactions that may cause an overdraft fee to be imposed on the accountholder? (staff commentary § 230.4(b)(4)-5)			
Transaction Limitations			
10. Do the account disclosures state any limits on the number or dollar amount of withdrawals or deposits? (§ 230.4(b)(5))			
Features of Time Accounts			
11. For time accounts, do the account disclosures also include the following, as applicable: (§ 230.4(b)(6))			
• The maturity date? (§ 230.4(b)(6)(i))			
A statement that a penalty will or may be imposed for early withdrawal, how it is calculated, and the conditions for its assessment? (§ 230.4(b)(6)(ii))			
• If compounding occurs during the term and the interest may be withdrawn prior to maturity, a statement that the APY assumes that interest remains on deposit until maturity and that a withdrawal will reduce earnings? (§ 230.4(b)(6)(iii))			
• A statement that interest cannot remain on deposit and that payout of interest is mandatory for accounts with the following features: (§ 230.4(b)(6)(iii))			
– Stated maturity is greater than one year,			
– Do not compound interest on an annual or more frequent basis,			
– Require interest payouts at least annually, and			
– Disclose an APY determined in accordance with section E of appendix A of Regulation DD?			
• A statement of whether or not the account will renew automatically at maturity? (§ 230.4(b)(6)(iv))			
– If the account will renew automatically at maturity, a statement of whether or not a grace period is provided and, if so, the length of the grace period?			
– If the account does not renew automatically, a statement of whether interest will be paid after maturity if the consumer does not renew the account?			
Bonuses			
12. Do account disclosures state the amount or type of any bonus, when the bonus will be provided, and any minimum balance and time requirements to obtain the bonus? (§ 230.4(b)(7))			

Regulation DD — Truth In Savings
Examination Checklist

	Yes	No	NA
Section 230.5 — Subsequent Disclosures			
Change in Terms Notice			
1. Does the institution provide advance change-in-terms notices to consumers advising them of any change to a term, required to be disclosed under section 230.4(b), that may reduce the annual percentage yield or that otherwise adversely affects the consumer? (§ 230.5(a)(1))			
• Does the notice include the effective date of the change? (§ 230.5(a)(1))			
• Is the notice mailed or delivered at least 30 days before the effective date of the change? (§ 230.5(a)(1))			
2. Are exceptions to the notice requirements limited to the following: (§ 230.5(a)(2))			
• Variable-rate changes? (§ 230.5(a)(2)(i))			
• Check-printing fees? (§ 230.5(a)(2)(ii))			
• Short-term time accounts (one month or less)? (§ 230.5(a)(2)(iii))			
Pre-Maturity Notices — Renewable Accounts			
3. For time accounts with maturities longer than one month and that automatically renew, does the institution: (§ 230.5(b))			
• Mail or deliver subsequent disclosures at least 30 calendar days before maturity of existing account? (§ 230.5(b)) (Alternatively, if a grace period of at least five calendar days is allowed, disclosures may be mailed or delivered at least 20 calendar days before the end of grace period.)			
• For accounts with maturities longer than one year, include in the disclosures: (§ 230.5(b)(1))			
– The account disclosures outlined in section 230.4(b) for the new account?			
– The date the existing account matures?			
– If the interest rate and APY for the new account have not been determined:			
1. The fact that the rates have not yet been determined?			
2. The date that the rates will be determined?			
3. A telephone number to call for the interest rate and APY that will be paid on the new account?			
• For accounts with maturities of one year or less, include in the disclosures: (§ 230.5(b)(2))			
– The account disclosures required under section 230.5(b)(1) for accounts with maturities of more than one year? (§ 230.5(b)(2)(i))			
OR			
– The date the existing account matures and the new maturity date if the account is renewed? (§ 230.5(b)(2)(ii)(A))			

Regulation DD — Truth In Savings
Examination Checklist

	Yes	No	NA
– The interest rate and APY for the new account, if known? – (§ 230.5(b)(2)(ii)(B))			
– If the rates are not known: (§ 230.5(b)(2)(ii)(B))			
1. The fact that the rates have not yet been determined?			
2. The date they will be determined?			
3. A telephone number to call for the interest rate and APY that will be paid on the new account?			
– Any difference in the terms of the new account, compared to the existing account? (§ 230.5(b)(2)(ii)(C))			
Pre-Maturity Notices — Nonrenewable Accounts			
4. For time accounts whose maturities are longer than one year and that do not automatically renew, does the institution: (§ 230.5(c))			
• Disclose the maturity date?			
• Disclose whether interest will be paid after maturity?			
• Mail or deliver the disclosures at least 10 calendar days before the maturity of the existing account?			
Section 230.6 — Periodic Statement Disclosures			
1. If an institution mails or delivers a periodic statement, do the statements include the following: (§ 230.6(a))			
• The "annual percentage yield earned" during the statement period, using that term and calculating the APYE in accordance with appendix A of Regulation DD? (§ 230.6(a)(1))			
• The amount of interest earned during the statement period? (§ 230.6(a)(2))			
• Any debited fees required to be disclosed under section 230.4(b)(4), itemized by dollar amount and type? (§230.6(a)(3)) **NOTE:** Except as required in section 230.11(a)(1) for overdraft payment fees, if fees of the same type are imposed more than once in a statement period, an institution may itemize fees separately or group them together and disclose a total dollar amount for all fees of the same type. Fees for paying overdrafts and for returning items unpaid are not fees of the same type and must be separately distinguished.			
• The total number of days in the statement period, or the beginning and ending dates of the period? (§ 230.6(a)(4))			
• If applicable, the total overdraft and returned item fees required to be disclosed by § 230.11(a). (§230.6(a)(5))			
If the institution uses the average daily balance method and calculates interest for a period other than the statement period, does the institution: (§ 230.6(b))			
• Calculate and disclose the APYE and the amount of interest earned based on the other period rather than the statement period?			

Regulation DD — Truth In Savings Examination Checklist	Yes	No	NA
• State the information required in section 230.6(a)(4), specifying the period length for the other period as well as for the statement period?			
Section 230.7 — Payment of Interest			
1. Does the institution calculate interest on the full amount of principal in the account each day using either the daily balance method or the average daily balance method? (§ 230.7(a)(1))			
2. For deposit accounts that require a minimum balance to earn interest, does the institution use the same method to determine any minimum balance that it uses to determine the balance on which interest is calculated? **NOTE:** An institution may use an additional method that is unequivocally beneficial to the consumer. (§ 230.7(a)(2))			
3. If an institution chooses not to pay accrued interest if the consumer closes an account prior to the date accrued interest is credited, does the institution disclose this practice in the initial account disclosures? (staff commentary §230.7(b)-3) **NOTE:** An institution is not required to compound or credit interest at any particular frequency but, if it does, it may compound or credit interest annually, semi-annually, quarterly, monthly, daily, continuously, or on any other basis. (§ 230.7(b) and staff commentary § 230.7(b)-1)			
4. Does interest begin to accrue no later than the business day specified for interest-bearing accounts in section 606 of the Expedited Funds Availability Act and implementing Regulation CC? (§230.7(c))			
5. Does interest accrue until the day the funds are withdrawn? (§230.7(c))			
Section 230.8 — Advertising Requirements			
General			
1. Do the types of advertising that the institution uses, including visual, oral, or print, meet the regulatory definition of an advertisement?			
2. Do the advertisements refrain from misleading or inaccurate statements, and from misrepresenting the institution's deposit contract? (§ 230.8(a)(1))			
3. Do the advertisements refrain from using: (§ 230.8(a)(2) and staff commentary § 230.8(a)-5)			
• The terms "free" or "no cost" (or similar term) if any maintenance or activity fee may be imposed?			
• The word "profit" when referring to interest paid on an account?			
• The term "fees waived" if a maintenance or activity fee can be imposed?			
4. If an electronic advertisement displays a triggering term, does the advertisement clearly refer the consumer to the location where the additional required information begins? (staff commentary § 230.8(a)-9)			

Regulation DD — Truth In Savings
Examination Checklist

	Yes	No	NA
5. For an institution that promotes the payment of overdrafts in an advertisement, does the advertisement include the disclosures required by section 230.11(b)? (§ 230.8(f))			
Permissible Advertisement Rates			
6. If the institution advertises a rate of return: (§ 230.8(b))			
• Is the rate stated as "annual percentage yield," using that term, and no other rate except "interest rate"?			
• If the advertisement uses the abbreviation "APY," has the term "annual percentage yield" been stated at least once in the advertisement?			
• If the advertisement states the interest rate, using that term, is it stated in conjunction with, but not more conspicuous than, the annual percentage yield to which it relates?			
• Are the annual percentage yields and interest rates rounded to the nearest one-hundredth of one percentage point (0.01%) and expressed to two decimal places?			
7. If the institution advertises tiered-rate accounts, does the advertisement state an annual percentage yield for each tier, along with corresponding minimum-balance requirements? (staff commentary § 230.8(b)-1)			
If the institution advertises stepped-rate accounts, does the advertisement state all the interest rates and the time period that each rate is in effect? (staff commentary § 230.8(b)-2)			
Required Additional Disclosures			
8. With the exception of broadcast, electronic, or outdoor media, telephone-response machines, and indoor signs, if the annual percentage yield is stated in the advertisement, is the following information, as applicable, stated clearly and conspicuously: (§ 230.8(c))			
• For a variable rate account, that the rate may change after account opening? (§ 230.8(c)(1))			
• The time period that the annual percentage yield will be offered, or a statement that it is accurate as of a specified date? (§230.8(c)(2))			
• The minimum balance required to earn the advertised annual percentage yield? (§ 230.8(c)(3))			
• For tiered-rate accounts, the minimum balance required for each tier stated in close proximity to and just as prominently as the applicable APY, if applicable? (§ 230.8(c)(3))			
• The minimum deposit to open the account, if it is greater than the minimum balance necessary to obtain the advertised annual percentage yield? (§ 230.8(c)(4))			
• A statement that maintenance or activity fees could reduce the earnings on the account? (§ 230.8(c)(5) and staff commentary § 230.8(c)(5)-1)			
• For time accounts, the following features: (§ 230.8(c)(6))			
– Term of the account? (§ 230.8(c)(6)(i))			

Regulation DD — Truth In Savings Examination Checklist	Yes	No	NA
– A statement that a penalty will or may be imposed for early withdrawal? (§ 230.8(c)(6)(ii))			
– A statement that interest cannot remain on deposit and that payout of interest is mandatory for noncompounding time accounts with the following features: (§ 230.8(c)(6)(iii))			
1. Stated maturity is greater than one year			
2. Interest is not compounded on an annual or more frequent basis			
3. Interest is required to be paid out at least annually, and			
4. The APY is determined in accordance with section E of appendix A.			
Bonuses			
9. Unless an exception applies in section 230.8(e), if a bonus is stated in an advertisement, does the advertisement state the following information, as applicable, clearly and conspicuously: (§ 230.8(d))			
• The "annual percentage yield," using that term? (§ 230.8(d)(1))			
• The time requirement to obtain the bonus? (§ 230.8(d)(2))			
• The minimum balance required to obtain the bonus? (§ 230.8(d)(3))			
• The minimum balance required to open the account, if it is greater than the minimum balance necessary to obtain the bonus)? (§ 230.8(d)(4))			
• When the bonus will be provided? (§ 230.8(d)(5))			
Exemptions for Certain Advertisements			
10. Do advertisements made through broadcast, electronic, or outdoor media, and telephone-response machines contain the following information, as applicable, clearly and conspicuously: (§ 230.8(e)(1) and staff commentary § 230.8(e)(1)(i)-1)			
• The minimum balance required to earn the advertised annual percentage yield? For tiered accounts, the minimum balance required for each tier stated in close proximity to and as prominently as the applicable APY, if applicable? (§ 230.8(c)(3))			
• For time accounts:			
– Term of the account? (§230.8(c)(6)(i))			
– A statement that interest cannot remain on deposit and that payout of interest is mandatory for noncompounding time accounts with the following features: (§230.8(c)(6)(iii))			
1. Stated maturity is greater than one year			
2. Interest is not compounded on an annual or more frequent basis			
3. Interest is required to be paid out at least annually, and			
4. The APY is determined in accordance with section E of appendix A of Regulation DD.			
• If an advertisement states a bonus:			

Regulation DD — Truth In Savings
Examination Checklist

	Yes	No	NA
– The "annual percentage yield," using that term? (§ 230.8(d)(1))			
– The time requirement to obtain the bonus? (§ 230.8(d)(2))			
– The minimum balance required to obtain the bonus? (§ 230.8(d)(3))			
11. Do indoor signs refrain from			
• Making misleading or inaccurate statement, and misrepresenting deposit contracts? (§ 230.8(a)(1))			
• Referring to or describe an account as "free" or "no cost" (or contain a similar term) if any maintenance or activity fee is charged?			
• Using the word "profit" to refer to interest paid on the account?			
• Using the term "fees waived" if a maintenance or activity fee can be imposed? (§ 230.8(a)(2) and staff commentary § 230.8(a)-5)			
13. If indoor signs state a rate of return, do they			
• State the rate as "annual percentage yield" or "APY"? No other rate may be stated except for the interest rate in conjunction with the APY to which it relates. (§ 230.8(e)(2)(ii)(a))			
Contain a statement advising consumers to contact an employee for further information about applicable fees and terms? (§ 230.8(e)(2)(ii)(b))			
Section 230.9 — Record Retention Requirements			
1. Has the institution retained evidence of compliance with Regulation DD, including rate information, advertising, and the providing of disclosures to consumers at the appropriate time (including upon a consumer's request), for a minimum of two years after disclosures are required to be made or action is required to be taken? For example, review samples of advertising and disclosures, policies and procedures, and training activities, as appropriate. (§ 230.9(c))			
Section 230.10 — RESERVED			
Section 230.11 — Additional Disclosure Requirements for Overdraft Services			
Periodic Statement Disclosures			
1. Does the institution disclose on each periodic statement (if it provides a statement and if a consumer is charged such fees) separate totals, for both the statement period and the calendar year-to-date, for the following: (§ 230.11(a)(1)and (2))			
• The total amount of fees and charges imposed for paying checks or other items when there are insufficient or unavailabile funds and the account becomes overdrawn, using the term "Total Overdraft Fees"? (§ 230.11(a)(1)(i)) (**NOTE:** The requirement to use the term "Total Overdraft Fees" is effective October 1, 2010) (§ 230.11(a)(1)(i)) **AND**			
• The total amount of fees and charges imposed on an account for returning items unpaid? (§ 230.11(a)(1)(ii))			

Regulation DD — Truth In Savings Examination Checklist	Yes	No	NA
2. Does the institution disclose the fees in close proximity to any fee identified in section 230.6(a)(3) that may be imposed in connection with the account and in a substantially similar format as found in Appendix B of Regulation DD? **NOTE:** The table must contain lines (or similar markings such as asterisks) inside the table to divide the columns and rows. (§ 230.11(a)(3))			
Advertisement Requirements			
3. Unless an exception under section 230.11(b)(2)-(4) applies, when an institution advertises the payment of overdrafts, are the following disclosed clearly and conspicuously in the advertisement:			
• The fee(s) for the payment of each overdraft? (§ 230.11(b)(1)(i))			
• The categories of transactions for which a fee may be imposed for paying an overdraft? (§ 230.11(b)(1)(ii))			
• The time period by which the consumer must repay or cover any overdraft? (§ 230.11(b)(1)(iii)) **AND**			
• The circumstances under which the institution will not pay an overdraft? (§ 230.11(b)(1)(iv))			
Disclosure of Account Balances			
4. If an institution discloses account balance information to a consumer through an automated system, does:			
• The balance exclude additional amounts that the institution may provide to cover an item when there are insufficient or unavailable funds in the consumers account? **NOTE:** The regulation does not require an institution to exclude funds from the consumer's balance that may be transferred from another account pursuant to a retail sweep program. (Staff Commentary ((§ 230.11(c)-2)) and (§ 230.11(c))			
• The institution, if it discloses at its option additional account balances that include such additional amounts, prominently state that the balance includes such additional amounts, and if applicable, that the additional amounts are not available for all transactions? (§ 230.11(c))			

Conclusions

Objective: Prepare written conclusion summaries, discuss findings with the EIC, and communicate findings to management. If necessary, initiate corrective action when policies or internal controls are deficient or when violations of law or regulation are identified.

1. Summarize findings and violations from the preceding procedural steps to assess the bank's level of compliance with the other consumer protection laws and regulations selected for review.

2. For those violations found to be significant or a pattern or practice, determine the root cause of violation(s) by identifying weaknesses in:

    *   Internal controls.
    *   Audit/independent compliance review.
    *   Training.
    *   Management oversight.
    *   Other factors.

3. Identify action needed to correct violations and weaknesses in the bank's compliance system, as appropriate. Determine whether reimbursements, civil money penalties (CMP), or an enforcement action should be recommended (refer to the CMP matrix).

4. Determine whether any items identified during this examination could materialize into supervisory concerns before the next examination (considering whether the bank has plans to increase monitoring in the affected area, or anticipates changes in personnel, policy, outside auditors or consultants, or business strategy). If so, summarize your concerns and assess the potential risk to the bank.

5. Determine the impact on the aggregate and direction of risk assessment for any concerns identified during the review (examiners should refer to guidance provided under the OCC's large and community bank risk assessment programs):

    *   Risk categories: compliance, transaction, reputation.
    *   Risk conclusions: high, moderate, or low.

- Risk direction: increasing, stable, or decreasing.

6. Provide the EIC with conclusions (discussing them with the EIC and, if appropriate, with the supervisory office), including:

   - Summary of violations.
   - Quality of risk management.
   - Quantity of risk (if this section was not completed during the exam, examiners should base their conclusions on the results of the quality of risk management procedures and the quantity of risk as identified by the bank's management information and control processes).
   - Recommended CMPs/enforcement actions, if any.
   - Potential reimbursements.
   - Recommended corrective action.
   - Recommended matters requiring attention (MRAs), which should cover practices that
     - Deviate from sound fundamental principles and are likely to result in financial deterioration, if not addressed, and
     - Result in substantive noncompliance with laws.

     MRAs should discuss
     - Causes of the problem.
     - Consequences of inaction.
     - Management's commitment to corrective action.
     - The time frame and person(s) responsible for corrective action.

7. Discuss findings with management. Obtain commitment(s) for corrective action as needed. Include in the discussion:

   - Quality of risk management.
   - Quantity of risk (include a listing of all violations, as well as significant violations).
   - MRA(s).

8. As appropriate, prepare a brief comment for inclusion in the report of examination.

9. Prepare a memorandum or update the work program with any information that will facilitate future examinations. Update the OCC electronic databases for all violations of law or regulation.

10. Organize and reference work papers in accordance with OCC guidance.